Beautiful you within me

TANYA TURTON

Copyright © 2020 Tanya Turton

Copyright remains the property of the author and apart from any fair dealing for the purposes of private study, research, criticism or review, as permitted under the Copyright Act, no part may be reproduced by any process without written permission. All inquiries should be made to the author.

Typeset & Cover by Chain of Hearts Creative

National Library of Australia - ISBN-9780648873921

When I look at me is it me that I really see?

These writings from source in all their knowing to be true are channelled for all of you in words we have witnessed the many of you to say.

"I AM LOOKING TO FIND THE REAL ME"

Is it this real version of you that you are to seek?

Or is it to improve the outer exterior version that you see. For let it be said that they are of two greater parts that are to be not equal in a sensing of this that you are. The limitations that are to be felt by those of you that are to think of yourself in this way as to be human in this form of which it is that the many of you present to all that you see as you, is incorrect into the thoughts of this that you should be. The greater existence of which it is that you reside into is to be the truest version of oneself that one must search inwardly to see of, for it is in this place of innermost love that you be that you will see the real you looking back for all to see.

We mirror that of thee upon herself being seen, for it is in this image that no mirror is needed into which one must see herself as to be. It is in this view to see, that you are the most beautiful you that we hold within us to be.

Seeing yourself for the true you
that you are to

Be.

It is of a wanting that we are to respond to, to hear in the many of you that are in this position of your now into which it is to ask.

In a simple belief as such this is to be, for it is in the many of you that it is to be seen forsaken, this that you are to see the beauty that is of you to be.

Beautiful
YOU WITHIN ME

"Beautiful You" let these two words fill you complete. In one's beauty of such to think, one will feel a hesitation to think of self to be, even a resistance to these words will be attached. For it is a truth for us to hear into that ones such as you have never let yourself speak or see of this physical you in this way. It's been too long has it not that you have viewed or thought of self in this way. If you have ever done so to be asked. Let it be reminded to you, by us the receivers of all your thoughts to be, that you are of this divine beauty that is to run so deep, shining upwardly and outwardly from within you to be felt first in an honest acceptance of this that you are to see yourself stand into to be then received. It is of this raw offering at first that feels oh so much to hurt, to see, to speak that your inner beauty will rise. One must be encouraged to close her human eyes to the physical seeing of it to be. For in the trust within you that speaks to offer here inlays your radiant beauty that one is to see to be discovered as this illuminating space that you are to shine into to offer. Let your inner beauty, your real beauty that we are ever present within you to see, to run deep and free to know of its value to be. And in your time, it will. For you are to be willing within to hear, to see as this beauty learns to speak. In the allowing of this beauty, to voice her love for you, it is then in this way to think that you will see the Beautiful You that is within Me.

In the transparent way in which one is to see of themselves in this self to be. One must be willing to remember of the great that lays embedded within them from the moment of conception in thought to be, to the ever guiding eternal voice within that lays steeped in wisdom so to speak of this great that is you in this very valuable moment of such your time to see into this that is you.

THE REFLECTION OF US TO BE SEEN WILL BE YOURS TO SEE ETERNALLY INTO.

CHAPTER ONE

LOOKING INTO THE LOOKING GLASS

The visions that ones such as yourselves are to hold dearly into, are to be often the most damaging to be felt in this reality of which it is to be presented for you. For often to stand to see of oneself in a truthful, loving way is felt by you that we are to witness often as a hard task to do. We witness to often the viewing by many if not all, the hardness to the external holder of the all that is complete within. For to appear to self as perfect in which it is that you are is to be not in your understanding of such to be,

Why is it in this we are to find ourselves not allowing of such to be?

To feel the closure of self to be surrounded by you to be, is to be in distrust or self-neglect of one such as yourself to be. For it is only of the earthly eye that peers at you, never seeing the real you only the external form as such to be. In the allowing of oneself to know the true reason of who it is that you be then in this view to envision one as willing to be seeing of all that lays great within is a must, for it is in here that we speak of the all that you are for us to see.

Allow us to help guide you into this loving path of oneself to be. For it has been written of this great love that you are to be willing and wanting and allowing of self to be. It is in this powerful statement that one is to sit into to know of, to hear of, to see of, and to feel of this magnificence that you are to be always in this that we are.

> *"Be the boldest that you can be, for you are the only one that we see in all that is to be of perfection within. It is not of your stance or outer structure that we concern to be, it is only in the knowing of this that is you to be love in all that you ask of us to be".*

It is the knowing of all that one is to feel within herself as she speaks her words and thinks of herself and the actions that she is to complete.

Why is it that it is to distress you so?

The thoughts that you think of are not yours to hold into or repeat to others for it is not so. We see into the all that you are to be and are asking of this to be heard that it is of you that we are. So, carry not of this dislike or distrust for it is not of us to allow. It is in only our gracious heart of hearts that belongs to us that we seek of you to be the true looker of oneself in this looking glass that only has a reflection back to you of love into oneself to see.

Stand brave you of big heart, for this reflection back, it is to show all that you carry as weakness and neglect within oneself for her in this looking glass. Love is only the rawness of which it is that one must see. For in this rawness is you we see, and it is of all that you think of to be flaws or disrupt let us say they are not. In all that you be being reflected back is the real you, the wanted you, the asking you to be this that you are so that you can cherish of this very moment of this that you are to become into. For this is your seeing of oneself and it is exactly as you intended it to be.

By the earthly eyes that hold of you this is of what you see but let us speak of only love for you. For if you are to rub clear that looking glass of all its moss and unforsaken stuff it will reveal to you a weeping eye of mistrust that is to be your self-looking back in the all that you thought of yourself to be, in the allowing of others to speak to and at you. For it is not of this image that you are to trust.

Take your time here, if you feel you can and….

Close your eyes sweet one and allow for the gentle voice of love to encompass you with want to be seen into this that you are to be the "Beautiful you within me".

WHY IS IT, THIS LOOKING AT ONESELF IN LOVE SO HARD TO DO?

It is in this present moment of this that you ask to see of yourself is it not? Then it is to say that all that you hold into oneself and onto for lack of elsewhere to place these thoughts into that one must rally up the courage we sense to say of this that looks back from the mirror to you.

"I wish to see the real me, for I am not of this that I think I see for I know that there is more to me than of what the physical eye allows me to see".

So, of you I ask,

I wish to see the real.....ME.

I wish to hear the real......ME.

I AM ME.

It is in this sensing of which one is to allow of, that all that you have lived in regret, loss, sadness and grief of what is not to be, is what it is that you see. It is not of the you that is glorious in this her present moment of now, for the past that is to linger in your thoughts, of loves lost and worries in deaths of ones that are to be and this sadness that sits inside of you for the you that you are not and the wanting of to be such that you see. These are the hardest things that we see to be for you to allow of them to be released into the all that we are.

Just ask we say, for we hear the many of you as you are to speak of this loss in a sensing of this that you are to be. It is not to be felt as lost upon your path or lost within self to be for this you are not.

When you are to gaze your eyes upon this presence that you see, know she is not lost this one that holds you strong from within, she is simply waiting on you to hear her sweet voice of love that is to be your sound to connect within this that is to be us.

In the greatest knowing of the one that you are to be is where you will find this that is to be you.

For there is to be no other that is as perfectly real as you.

No need to hang your head or shut this book to close as we speak, for we are willing to see you in only this form that you be. It is she that is to shine to us in a loving way so as not of you that we are to forget. This life that you exist into has been heard and understood only by the voice that lives inside your head for this is the voice that does not listen to the her that you are guided by. For this voice of contempt is to win all wars in wager of the love that you are to be. For it does not listen willingly, for it is to not trust of this that you speak.

In love it says, in jest you are not worthy of this we hear ones such as yourself to speak, your form within is perfection in its radiance and if you listen closely to this voice of love that we speak you will see the change from within to seep outwardly to the all that you are to be in this that we see of you to become your view of you.

It is out of the moss that one is to grow, her roots so deeply planted this she is to know, it is the tenderness of new growth that we are to see, for they are to stretch to the shining heavens above her. To be felt upon her tender self as she is to grow. It is in this knowing that it is to be felt, as her roots so tender stretch deep to be that she must allow of all that she is to feel of this that she has become. And in this knowing of such to be that she will reach the heavens to say that this is she once again. More she has become.

We speak in truth of the allowing of such that you are to be in a position of love to view oneself into. For this is hard we are to observe for most if not all that are, are to think of themselves as not. It is to forfeit the longing of such that you be to the realms of all that is to exist within oneself to be for it is in this way in which to view that you will see the true reflection of you.

Allow for the noticing of such that you're not for it is extended and exaggerated here in these eyes that you view, it is not easy this we offer. The human form is complex in her thoughts of such herself to be. It is in this way that we view, when all is coated in love to be viewed that one's such as us that are of you are to witness the transformation of this rough exterior to be debarked so that you can be in this space to be ever present of the you that is looking back at you. It helps this we know to review of all that you have to say for there is often much that holds you back regarding the form you are too rough to hold. It is of these spoken words whether in jest or contempt for you they are too real it is to hear of this that you think is to be.

The softening that is to begin within this that you are, for she is to be gentle to the spoken heart that is asking of her true self to be. Stand timidly it is to feel of one in this space to ask, for all your words are heard let this be offered to you. The changing of conversations within and externally are the ones that we are to ask for you to see, it is in these words of harsh disgust and in a diminishing need to be that you are responding into to be.

What is it that you see?

We see of only love. In this it feels surreal for the eyes that see and the mind that thinks both are unable to feel this trust that you are not of what it appears to be. It is unlimited this view of you that we see. Respond into this that we offer to you to think for it is of you that you are tied into the connection of one to be.

So it is in this that we say that all is complete in every way although it does not feel it is of us to trust for in this relationship of love that is a must you will feel the growing form within to be this that you are to hear, that all is fine and just in this that you are to be.

Much seeking is done to unravel the need to be of another or even just to be better than you are not. Some may say this is a good thing to be present within for to strive to be is always allowing of someone to be seen. It is not of this that we disagree but it is the way in which the human mind is to think of this to be, for the allowing of growth comes out of the finding of this love within you to be allowed to be accepted in a truth of kind that you really are to be. We seek not of one to rally into this to be profound within for it is in the asking of you to be found that you seek too deep within. For the flow of us that is to be spoken of in this gentle way is to be the true sense of direction that you will find your way. Many will wander and feel lost within her way of the seeing and the believing of this that she is to be.

The search appears endless and hard to trust does it not?

For it is of what you are looking for to be that becomes the nagging doubt within that you will never find to be of. It is in this that we wish to offer to you to know, all that radiates from within is brighter than you will ever know. So, discard this physical forms thoughts of such to be and allow for all that flows into you to be the thoughts of wisdom, grace and the conscious being of love that you be and it will fill you up in this intensity of this that you are to be. Allow for this to be a recognition within no matter how slow it needs to be for it is in this knowing of such and these words of just that you are to feel the change occurring deep within.

We have followed you intensely upon this journey that you have become and some agreed to be in need for more than they can hold into oneself to be, it is in all that try to be that are and in this asking of such that you will be again in your entirety of to be.

We see of you often in lacking thoughts to be for you are too worrisome of this that you are. Stand square and front on when you see of all that you be for it is not to turn away in disgust or despair for you are as you are to be seen. It is in the holding on of all that you are to feel as though it is of yours to see into that allows this form to be remiss in her thoughts of this that she is.

It is in love that we are to only see, for all that appears to be wrong within is heard and we disagree for the truth is to be felt to be said that you are of this greatness that we feel of you within.

CHAPTER 2

ALLOWING ONESELF TO DE-FLUFF

We see of you as you are to see this image of you that you are not, for it is of us to know of this that you think of yourself to be. It is in the looking upon oneself in lack of that you appear to be.

What is it that you think you should be?

Search not into another or those that you see for they too are in this space of which to judge upon all that they see? It is in this here that is yours to fear for she is to be held into here and it is in this that you must trust. The fluff we say that you would call baggage to be carried is to be allowed to be felt as just that, it can be put down and allowed to rest if you are to be in a position of such to do this.
It would do you just.

We offer a vision here of you to see standing in front of a looking glass to see for it is in this that you do so hesitantly.

We watch as you judge, squeeze, criticise, poke and prod, the voice that we hear is to be said unjust.

Kind words are needed here, and it is of your own voice that you need to hear. For it is often of another that you are to repeat words that have been said. Gently hold your thoughts as they are to be, for they too will want to vanish into this to be of those that you think of yourself to be. It is a gentle unfolding that one must start to begin for you are this you that you see, superb in all that you be within. It is the physical form that carries much doubt of the trust that you know to find within when you are to get out of this mind and thoughts that you be. It is in oneself that you are to allow for thoughts of love gentle and kind, this may feel alien to you to use in this sensing of oneself to be. Repeat after me….

I AM WORTHY OF THIS LOVE TO BE.

The times that have felt as not right for you it is of a many we have seen. It is in this life that you have lived that you have chosen to be. It is in this sensing of oneself to be this that you are carrying along to be. Feel yourself in this wanting to be stripped bare and raw so that only you can see, for there is nothing that you are carrying that is of need for you to be. It lingers this we know in many moments of unjust and distrust fraught with envy and sadness of what it is that you appear not, but you are to begin in this space as it appears to you to be.

Slowly, loving, gentle and caring for it is not of another that must. It appears to us to be you the sensor in all this that is to be that you will stand before oneself to see and look upon this looking glass to see the beautiful you that lays within me.

'Free the fluff' it is to be said for it all lingers too easily in this that you speak of in the many words that you've said. Feel yourself start to vibrate from within in the small words of encouragement that you are to offer, watch as this fluff frees itself from your shell, for in this fluff lays doubt of this that you are to be. Wash clean your thoughts of this to be yours for it is there if you need it to be. But trust us to say that it serves you better if you leave it up to us to eliminate it into dust. If you still require it to be after thoughts of you as this to be, you can attach it again still the same.

In eagerness one is to begin this new challenge to become.

May we suggest that it doesn't happen overnight and the harder your thoughts to this that you are to apply the more you need to trust. It is of this word you see that has allowed the many of you to depart from the true love that you are and the person that you must trust in the most.

Start small we say in everyday be proud to stand correct in thoughts of this that I AM.

The sensing of such to be found within is the love that you be.

Guidance is needed and is with you in every way.

All that you feel is your own correct way.

Sense into this being of love that you are, be ignorant to those that offer you too much to say.

Timidly one looks for it is often in this viewing that you have forgotten of the real you that you are to be. The covering, the altering, the pretending, the changing of you to be something that you are not is to be a process over time that you have allowed to become.

Being blinded by thoughts of this that you are not for they are heavy and burdensome in all that they are felt within this that you are. To carry of this is too much to bear, of this it is that we know, and it is to cripple those of you that are in what it feels like no state of repair. It is of us to guide you here to say that all that you are to offer us is heard in every way. Allow for the voice of self-neglect to be quietened in all words that she is to have said. If words of genuine calm cannot be said, then it is better to offer none instead. Grow a sense of willingness within so that you may feel as this voice of peace is to rise within slowly offering to you this that you be instead.

We hear you asking, what shall be said, and will I hear of it to be spoken?

Your words are so often designed in your head, these are to be the ones felt so deeply cutting and hurtful within this form that you be. It is the voice that whispers softly at first almost hard to be heard, for she is the wise one within and knows of her time to speak for you to hear of her to become once again. She whispers silently it feels at first. For this we

have heard by the many of you that have offered this to us that it is not of a voice that I hear.
What is wrong with me? Why can I not hear?

Know that this voice is to be felt first within your heart, this heart is yours to trust and know of all that she has to say will be heard. The heart is covered and dullened in thoughts of love to be for so many of you are often hurt so deeply within this heart space to feel that one is not in any way, state or form to negotiate within this that one is to feel.

WE sense a sadness become of this one that appears lost.

We, us, spirit, source, god in your choosing of us to be felt are in this righteousness to know of all that you are, it is never to be felt lost for you are not.

In the allowing of others to guide you so it is to be seen by those of us to offer that they do not steer your boat. You as humans, you appear to like the sense of another to steer you to this that you are to appear to be. Getting lost among those that are of unjust within themselves to appear, for they too are searching deeply of others to hear into this that they have to say, and it is in this that you must not. For their voice is to be no bolder than your own. It is to be offered here that yours is to be heard more in the correctness for you to hear.

Sensing of the one within

We see of you standing here in this space that is to be thought of as yours, thoughts aplenty running wildly and indecisively around into your head. Allow of these thoughts to be known to you for they are offering to you such in an answer to oneself of the things that you are to not need to know of. If it is to linger a fraction to long in regards to this that you think of, than it is to be allowed to be dismissed as a thought of not wanted and is in your allowing of such to be asked out loud for this thought to be no longer in needing of your thoughts to be.

'Please take this thought from me'

In these thoughts to be not wanted you will feel the heaviness and confusion as they are to continually roll over and over in a mental struggle to release them. In comparison to the flow of thoughts that are to be encouraging and limitless. For they will flow continual into that of another that is to grow into a space of free flow to feel the intention of these to be of a wanting to watch as they progress into this that they are to be an encouragement from within you to be.

In the asking, becomes sensing of this magnificent ever knowing being of love that you are to be heard, for she is to be seeing all of this that you put before her, but in such a way of which it is to understand that it is not for you to need.

Allow for yourself to sit in peace and calm for even just a moment of time it appears to us that you as humans find this undoable in most sensing of oneself to be allowing of such to be. It has been offered here to us, to hear of that in ones inability to sit into a quiet reserve of space to allow for self to be heard, it feels to those of you that try, you try too hard and are in too much asking of the answers to be delivered in this very moment of introspection of self to begin. This we offer to you to know that it will not appear to you in this exact moment of so wishing of it to be, for the time of its true revelation within oneself will be of a so choosing of souls ability to remember when it was upon this you were to know of.

In allowing for the sensing of self to be; we offer to you here to feel into that one must be diligent into thoughts of them self to be of love and kind, gentle moments of tenderness in regards to the words they are to speak of themselves and of another. For this is to become apparent to oneself that it all shall flow from within to the outer-ness of this that you will find another to be listening to receive.

The sensing of self feels nondescript in thoughts of how too and it is in this asking of by those of you that we are to witness into will feel the need to ask then ignore or misplace this desire, for it feels like to heavy a task to begin to let alone see a finish.   Let us offer to you all here in this that you are to listen. It is in the sensing of this magnificent light within to be heard as the trusting self to be the true asker. For it is not words of the human voice that is heard but when the human heart, the life force within you asks, then it shall be heard.

The heart space to hold so intently this love is often felt to be boarded over in a sense of protection against all that it has held dear to self and been lost and misplaced. This allows for us to speak of, it will soften and down grade all feelings of this that does not fit into this calling of love to be. For it is in this space that the true sensing of self will rise to be met by you in this form of such that you are to be.

See only of self in this view to be, for the exterior that you look upon is not... It is to be seen in this vision of self to be for only this part of this journey that you have become. It is into this form that you see that the true you are to be, and she is to know of this that she will become again to be seen in another image of self to be. She fears not of her eternalness and the place that she shall arrive into. For she is of greatness. Knowing of this that she is divine within. So, you see this is to offer that all that you think of yourself. You are not. It is in the hardened form of thoughts that you feel into and often fake to see. Feel the resistance of self to release this exterior mould that you be so that you may feel first to see with the eyes that see of all that you are.

The real version of self in this light of completeness that you are.

What do I see when I see me?

We would offer here for you to hear of this that we speak of, that in the seeing of oneself in this the human form is to be no different to that in which it is that you would see another, would it not?

For it is often the judging eyes of lust, jealousy, hope, greed and distress that ones such as yourself are to view of self and others, is it not?

This form that looks back from within you in her ability to see of this that she is in this form to be, (meaning here to be said your spirit, source, light form within) is to know of the likeness that you (in the physical) does not as yet see of all that are to present to you in the formatting of such that they are, (your divine guides, loves and spirit in its true essence to be).

All that one is to see, is to be seen in this perfect vision of which it is that we(spirit) are to see you all in.

When I look, I do not see this of myself to be.

Trust of us to offer in this that you will. For all that be are to sense this knowing within that you are to be more of this than you are. You will start to see the smallest of glimmers of this light extruding from within to begin to notice the shifts that one is to feel in the human form to be felt as a retaliation against this whim of desire that it be to see of oneself in a more familiar loving pattern.

Yes, it is of us to offer to you that this is the correct stage of movement within that you will begin to trust oneself to feel, this movement is small, cautious and gentle this we say but allow for it to move within and it shall. It is not of oneself to feel as though they are to commit to an offering as such to us or that they may feel inadequate in the sensing of self to be, for it is to rise upwardly and outwardly from you in often the times of such unexpected knowing of this to be felt.

> For your time has been acknowledged by your soul as this is the time to feel, to ask of this movement to begin within once more. It is always in the knowing of such to be and this you are to allow for it just to be. No doing it is that we say, only of the one must do to speak of and that is to see yourself and all that you are to see of in

We speak of this great offering to be, so that all that one must be is to know lays intently within self.

It is not new to us to view you in this format that you are for you have presented to us in many times before all in the same space, time, and reality of this to be seen into. For you are to be knowing of this that you are just in a space of which it appears this time again to be forgotten.

We seek into you to define this disturbance within so that she may feel of us lingering in a sense of eagerness to be heard. For our voice of one is the most powerful of all that is to speak and it will be heard in this that you are to listen to our words of commitment, love and grace into all that you choose to become again and again.

For it is to be offered that our voice does not appear different to the many that are choosing of such it to be heard. We are all in the coherent state of which it is that we speak of the many realising's of such that you have become. But it is to appear that all our voices are to speak as the one that is to be seen in all, the creator of source in the greatness that it is to be and this voice of one is to be felt and heard in all its sensing of to be you this that we speak of.

CHAPTER 3

IN YOUR VOICE I HEAR

"The hearing of us is impossible to hear" we hear of this in your many voices to offer to us to be heard into.

Yes! This we agree for the asking so often overlaps the real reasoning behind the questions that are asking of this to be heard into. WE are ever knowing of this that be your spirit within, and we know of her voice to speak in love and of love and that in the difference of the human voice that wants. The voice that is chosen as yours to hear is really yours to know of, for it appears to those that are to listen as to be of their own that they hear into deep.

The many of you that are wanting of this voice out of ego or sensing of themselves still not to be, will hear nothing of this sweet voice of love that we are to be heard into. It is the extremes that many of you will go to that we are to witness in the finding or ability of self to hear of this voice that they crave so hard to hear. It is in these human components of self that one is to find the searching of self to begin and this is often where the first steps of this so-called journey of this life is to begin.

We offer to you all that our voices are to be heard in their eternalness of them to be. But is only heard in the asking of true forgiveness and want of this that you are to be found within. For she is not of one to hide but is to lay dormant if to offer a word here to speak of that she is wanting of this to be heard, to be spoken and of the true knowing of all that she is to be of. She will find her voice once again into this that we be so that all that you are needing of which to hear of will be heard loud and clearly for you to hear into and speak so defiantly of this love that is to be.

In the wanting to hear of this voice so desperately I am often told that I am trying too hard.

How does one overcome this trying to hear and allow for it to soften within us?

Let us offer to you here to be heard that it has been said in many conversations with you that in the trying to be something that you are not or do not have is where the lesson or so the giving is to be not of an ability to see.

It is in the human mind that one is to want of and to have not, it is to be thought of as a missing or lacking is it not? So, it is in here that we are to present to you that all that we see of is correct within those of you that are to ask and of those that do not. It is to be offered to you to say that in the hearing of this voice that we are, of this voice that you are of, is in all its eternity of to be just you.

So, in the understanding of this to be you, to be able to be in a position of such to hear of this voice which in truth is simply yours to be. Although it is in this true hearing that all masks, veils and coverings and lies of self are to be released into this that we are. For it is in the true sensing of self to be and the prominent allowing of self to be really seen as this that you truly are, this is when the first of tiny whispers are to become a wanting within self to hear. Let us guide you here into this knowing of one's own true voice for it is to begin softly.

Yes! This we say and it will depend on your willingness to hear in trust of self to be that will determine its volume for you to hear. It is in this tiny voice that has the chance to escape the humanoid that it is to sit into and if you are willing in your ability to hear, it is this tiny voice of yours that will feel as though she is to corrupt all that you hold into yourself as yourself to be. For it is in amongst this corruption of self that it is that you will feel the falling of resistance by the one that you think is to be your thoughts and your mind to be. Let us offer they are not. Useful we offer into this that you are to need as a human functioning upon this planet to be in this life that you are yes, we give you that, but useless really in the true knowing of self to be heard.

What must one do to allow for this transformation within to take place?

We see it not to be thought of as a transformation to be for it is not. It is in the common sense of self to be that one is unable to be allowing of this voice to be heard. It is often in the thinking human mind that you are to focus so intently upon the truth of this existence that is to feel commonplace within ones such as yourself to think of us to be of something rather than not. We say this to offer to those of you that are to think of us to be not relevant within oneself and in this offering, one must allow for the thinking mind to become complacent shall we say as to think of us to be. When human eye can only see to believe then to believe in the unseen it becomes a challenge to the thinking mind for this to be allowed within to feel true. It is the thinking mind that is strong within this form that you are and if it is not to be witnessed or thought of in this way than it is likely that all that you are wishing to become into once more will eventuate. It is of the human will power that the minds strength is to be seen as the strongest component into thoughts of such not to be. And it is in this we ask you to let go of all thought's of this that you are, so that you may offer a willingness to become a sensing within self to be of this that they are to appear as to be not.

Feel not as though you are not of an important existence in this form that you are to present to us in this life, for you are. And it is in this form of all that we are proud to say we sit easily and interpreting of such that you are, and it is revered amongst us all in this that we are to see you. But it is in these faults of yours that you have allowed for the human mind to become your sense of wisdom to know. This we offer it is the wrong organ that has been chosen in this life of the most of you to witness in your choosing of such that you are to be. Let us offer here to say that the human heart that is lit from within with this tiny spark that is to remain always illuminate to us, it is to be allowed to be seen as the true communicator of all that you are to be within us eternally.

IN THIS CHANNELLING OF WISDOM, IT IS THAT I OFFER...

In the want to hear of us from the egotistical form that is to reside in you, is where the many distrusts and mistruths have been allowed to be offered to those of you that are in your honesty of self and are to be truly looking to seek of us to be heard.

Allow not of another and in this we offer to speak of that in words that are spoken of here in this space that you are to connect into are your words of truth, form, and the justice that resides within you to speak of them to be heard.

We offer that in this source of flow the words of correctness can be felt. So, in the sensing of self to be one must allow for all forms of such that are to feel heavy upon oneself in the information that they are to offer, (for many channels of self-disrupt are and have been allowed to flow into oneself from that of another that is to offer to you making them your choosing of such words to be).

This we are to put right within you that all that are to speak are of their own knowing and thoughts of such that we are to be. But in this that you are wanting of to hear is to become your own knowing of the real us that we are. No voice of another is to be your true speaker or guider of such that you are to become. It is in the unwilling mind of thought that the many of you are to offer to those that are to speak for you to grasp this that we are. You will hear only of their voices and not of your own. This we add that this voice that you think to listen to in these writings that are to be presented; are yes received by this channels understanding of such that she is to be and it is in this receiving of such that she is to receive that we are to find of her to be a clear channel of thought so that all that she is to interpret is to be presented in her exact knowingness of this that she is to feel into.

So let it be said that all that is spoken of in offering in this space of recognition that one is to sit into today is of truth, justice and love that is to be felt within the all of you that are in the choosing of self to be.

Can we not impart upon all of you this knowledge of which is yours to receive into?

That the one voice that speaks for the many of us here in these realms of existence are yes, the experienced warriors of your time and times long since departed, the builders of all that you see into in this time of yours to be past, present and future, the knowledgeable tutors that have spoken so intently within themselves to be heard, the seers, the true Christ, the buddas, the gods and goddesses and the wise men and women of ancient tribes and civilisations that have sat in this beautiful place of which it is to recognise of us to be of them, and the many truths that have come before you. You are meant to know of them to be for they all searched and became knowingly into this place that you are to be. It is to be seen into all that we are the eternal universal travellers of this the holders of this wisdom of those that are to experience all of the knowing that is to be, for we are ever and always the true guiders as such and we are the true voice of you when it is desired within oneself to speak and it is of us that you are to be.

One is to feel this that they are to know within themselves to feel, that all that you are to see of us is different in all sensing of us to be. WE are true for our forms are not limited to such that we see of your beliefs into this that we are to be known to you as. We are an aspect of self to be first remembered as one to be and in this feeling within it is to be the contrast of all that you are to recognise yourself as to be different to us to be seen. The heavy outer-ness that is your form to choose into one will feel to notice that we are not of this way to be. In your allowing of us to be generated into your thoughts you will feel us represented in many different images, faces, looks and energies, these are all comprised of the ever knowing within our being of love that we are to be and any form that you as the seer so desire of us to see into you will. In the sensing of such to be guides, angels, gods, etherical beings and colours of distinction to recognise are to just name a few for we are all into this that we are to be and that is to be known as the ever loving source that is the will and completeness of all that is.

True to ourselves one must always be for there is no other like you to exist, in this one must know that you are all of the same in this uniqueness that is to be recognised as this that we are of

ONE.

CHAPTER 4

FEELING THE FLOW WITHIN

One is to not seek of this flow for it is already within. It is in this asking of this flow to show itself to you that it will. Be certain of this. It is of this that we are to know of and in this trusting of self that is to be heard within it shall be shown to you. This flow that we speak of is to be questioned by the many of you that are to ask and of those that sit-in disbelief of whether it is possible to be so.

This flow is to be felt within as like a never ending feeling of peace, calm and excitement that is to contain the everyday thoughts of self-neglect, distrust and lack of within oneself so that all that is not to serve is in the position to be able, to be accepted as knowledge from within and you as the asker of this love to be within you found.

You will watch as the observer of all that you are to be only of in this format of such to be seen as human and watch with loving eyes of this that is not of your own good is allowed to be seen in the eyes of love that are true within you and are allowed to be part of this magnificent flow. For this flow does not hold onto anything. As all in its presence of oneself, is to be found into and in this knowing of this to be made apparent to self. It is to feel as a humbleness of distraction to the thoughts of self to be that all that is not of your worthiness is allowed to be offered to the external ethers of us that we so shall reside into. For it is in this residing of such that you think of us to be is not of thoughts to be far away for we are relevant within the all of you that are to speak of us to know. For we are the willingness that you have chosen into to know of your existence to be truth within you to be.

The fight within oneself is to become apparent to self through this that we are to hear you call the journey of self-discovery. This flow is a never to be forgotten part of the soul and the spirit but is to be forgotten so knowingly, yet unwillingly by the human that you have become into. One is to learn upon this place, to know of self to be once again that the true knower that is to reside within is to be allowed to remind you of this to be.

In the splitting of self from there lays the choices that one is to make for it is to feel as though upon the witnessing of spirit and soul to be heard within you, this is to allow for the human form to think of self to be that of another this we say you are not. It is in the stronger desire of self to be that does not allow for the spirit to be seen ever so knowingly like she or he shall be, so the continual fight within this human way to think of and the non-resistant fight from within that usually the human being is to be the winner. This we have to offer it is to be patient for the true you that is all of this that you are is to be heard in your timing of such to be for it was planted directly within you this time of unravelling to be. It is in this that you are searching of to be that it shall become.

The hardness that one in human form is to feel to allow of this flow to exist is to be seen by us as the incomplete acceptance of this that you are to be of us. For we are plenty this you should know and our connections with the many of you that are to ask is widely and suggestively growing. It is to be seen by us that the emotions of the human form are the true holders of such this to be seen as grief and a sadness within of this not to be.

Let us correct you here in this that be your now of which it is to know of that you are all in this courageous position of which it is to hear. It is to be seen as your gravest desire within oneself to hear of us, yet it is the human conditioning of such to be a human upon this planet that this feeling of contentment is hard to grasp. It is that your thoughts are to be ruled by the many that are to feel as though you are not to know of this that is to be you. Love! Yes, Love, is the ruling component of our universal desiring of you to become into once again. Seek not of others to allow your knowledge of this love to grow for this love that is your true love is designed within you to flow into the correct receiving of yours to be in the asking of such that it shall be once more.

Is there a way for me to explore into this love without feeling trapped into something that I may not want to be?

Yes, all that search are to be considered the true explorer of self within, is this not so to feel.

If one is to follow only their own true guidance of thoughts of us to be then and only then you will feel the gentle pull from within to sit into this space of recognition of it to be. This is to be found in the many of you searching of us to be. In this gentle space of love and connection of self to be allowing for the voice that you hear of the feelings that you are to feel into and the light that one will eventually see become the true guiders of self-intuition as such to be called that you are in the right space of wanting. Are you not?

It is not of a place to hold oneself into if they do not wish it to be, for your wariness of this space is often the answer of this space to not feel open to self to sit into. Let us say that in one's ability to trust into this that we are and of the love that you will be once more attuned into that you will feel of this space to be only of warmth and a knowing of such that you are to be ever present within.

It is not of our wishing that you are to feel trapped into a place that does not feel correct within you. So, it has been established within self before this day that you were presented to earth to be that you would not feel of this recognition as such to be of yours until the so chosen time of it to

BE.

If one is to work or study at this connection to be developed, will it come quicker to the seer of it to be?

It is in the workings of this to be that one is to feel the stresses of the external life that you live into to be of a chore or task of such that we are to understand to know of to offer to you to be. It is in the seeing of oneself to work or study upon these thoughts of such to be that the logical mind is to present to you the workings of such that you are not. It is in this knowing of self to be exquisite, in the true self regarding these asking's of her to be. For one must not work at this as to be thought of as a task or chore as such for it is to be allowing of oneself to be gentle in all that she spends her time in the self-adjusting of the innerness that you be in this space that you are to connect into.

This space that we speak of is yours and ours that are to be felt in a connection of sorts to be. It is a powerful yet gentle place to sit this is to be said that this is your place of recognition within of all that be. So to feel as if this is a chore to be completed or worked into is to be seen by us a failure of to feel within oneself as to not be in a position of which it will be to feel of this that you are searching within for. It is to flow ever so naturally within, and the question often asked of is:

What am I to think of all that I am to receive?

This we offer nothing. For all that is, is of your own intention to be as such of you to be of us, and it is in this flow to be of no holding into that one will transpire further and deeper into one's own self recognition of us to be. Do not place a title or thought upon what it is that you see for all that you see is of you in the greatest reveal of you to be. Allow for the coming of it to be yours to witness into, and feel not the need to share of this to others. These are your own self empowering thoughts of this that we are for you to feel into and all will be continued into if this is allowed to flow freely with no intentions of distrust to be.

What if I feel my flow to be blocked?

One's flow is to be told of as this, it is never blocked for you are always a continuation of this that we call source to be. It is often in the human mind to think of this life as hard and not of your wanting that thoughts are to arise within you that you will feel as though you are not entwined still within this bigger being of love that you be. It is hard, this we admit being of human in thoughts and yet have a great desire welling up within you to remember of this spirit that you are to hold within. For it is the human sensing of self to be in disregards of such that you could possibly be in such a knowing of all times is perfectly understood to us in this timeframe that you sit into.

It is when one begins to notice of these thoughts that are to flitter through your thinking mind that one is to become apparent of the search within to the thoughts and of what it is that they are attached to, if anything that is to be of purpose to you to think into. It is the human body's ability to forgo all thoughts of this that is spirit to be the true light that they see of self within that one has decided to undertake as the being of such that you be into this human form. For it does not feel important to the physical self in this form to be of this that is your now of which to think of yourself as one that is resilient to these human thoughts and emotions that can easily deter you from the light shining within. Yes, it is this we are to admit that the challenge for you even though it shall not be seen as this, for it is to hinder your thoughts of love in every way possible. This daily grind as you would put words to it to be, is to be seen only in the love that you asked of yourself to discover into and to find out of this that you are living into to be of a learning as such of the magnificent being within to be. This was asked so that she can continue upon her path of trials and tribulations to be of this that she so desired of herself to become her knowledge of them to be learnt here upon this planet known as Earth.

For she will not and does not see of you to be one that is blocked off from her to see. It is in her deepest knowing of which it is to understand into that she is willing in every way that is to be presented to you to see and feel into to allow for your thoughts to be of hers so that you may find just in this becoming of self to be.

CHAPTER 5

THE SLEEPING GIANT WITHIN

Feel your awakening within, to release the sleeping giant that holds ALL this love within her heart.

Be bold in your sensing of this sleeping giant that is to lay within for this is us in all that we are to be. It is in this heaviness that one is to feel within of this sense of wanting to know but unsure to speak of.

It is in this time of your realisation into this question that one is to ask of this that we are and how to get in touch to receive. It is for you to know of this that we are to know that this sleeping giant does not lay deterred, for she is simply quiet to all aspects of self until the realisation of self is to be enabled to be visioned as more than the physical that she is to be. It is in the asking that all that this giant is to hold of in wisdom, courage and most importantly of this love that is hers to envision yourself to be in. It is in this sleeping giant that lays content within this form that you are ever gentle in her guidance of self to be, for it is in this continual ever knowing contact of all that she be that she will not feel the need to rise unless the desire of self within is to feel of this connection in this form that she be.

It is in the gentle persuasion of thoughts that are given and offered to ones such as yourself to be thought of in a sense of recognition of more than of what it is that you are to be in this physical realm, that you will feel this need to ask of this question.

Who and What am I?

The deepest of rumbles are to be felt as a gentle stirring within this form that you are and it is to shake the belly and move the heart with a knowing of such that you are present in all that you be. So that you may see of this that we are to offer to you at once to feel of this giant to awaken. Fear not of this wording as giant to be, for to envision the size of something to be huge or enormous than this is to rationalize this form of us to be in an understanding of this capacity of which it is that we exist into.

For we are known to the many that are to have woken this giant within for the greatest potential of self to be recognised into for upon one's own asking it shall be. It is of us to know of this to be as such that one is to ask for the giant to be realised into ones thoughts of this to know and it shall be offered here to know of that this giant is to fill you completely with the sensing of all that you are.

It is to fear not of this giant that we speak of for it is of us that we refer this statement to and all that we are is to be received in an honesty of self in the wanting of such to be known from within once more. The many of you that are willing and in understanding of this that we speak of, are to allow for this giant to rise on up and fill you complete from within. So that all that you may feel to offer is the purest of sensing of this giant to be only of love and kindness that is to be offered to all that you see. Fear not the trapping of such within for it is not of a trapping that we see ourselves to be. It is only upon ones realising of this that they are to ask into that they will feel of this that we are to be true to your sensing of this that we ask of you to be remembered into.

Seek not of another's thoughts to be for your giant of intoxicating ever offering love is all involved within you this we know. And it is in this understanding of thought to be that you will come to feel the stirrings and movement within self so intently that one is to ask of more so that they can better know of this not so sleeping giant. Watch as you expand here into this that you are feeling. Allow this giant to become, for it is of you that you are to have asked of self's soul to be reminded of this that is to appear. A timid gentle love of self to accept to start the full-blown realisation of such that we are of you once more that you will feel intently.

We have heard it spoken to say, that there is no one that can or will derail me from this knowing in this lifetime that I am present in this my now.

GIANT

- An imaginary or mythical being of human form but superhuman size.
- A person of exceptional talent or qualities
- A star of relatively great size and luminosity.
- Of very great size or force.

It is of all this that we are to represent. For you see in the inner eyes of the beholder to speak it is to be offered here to say that all that you think to be will. Free your limitations of such that you are to be and allow for the giant within you to be an imaginary and mythical sensing of self to be full of this magic as such that you are to be known. Let all your talents and qualities be allowed to unfold for these are of yours to have agreed. This star that is to shine so bright from within is yours to spill over and out of you to be seen for we are to never lose sight of thee. Our size and force as such to be exerted upon oneself in the form of an understanding of us to be is in your own thoughts of allowing of all that we be just this, that we are in all forms thought of and presented to you to think of us to be. Let it be bold in thoughts of this giant that we are to be. To speak of a giant as such is to be only seen in the eyes of the beholder as an opening within of such magnitude and universal in size to allow for the realising of this LOVE that is bold, that we are, is always of you to be.

CHAPTER 6

WANTING MORE

It is true we are to say that in the receiving of us to be felt within, leaves the receiver of no doubt as such that we are to energise and fill ones whole with such of a completeness to be that it is for us to see that you as the self are always to want more.

As I sit here in the wonderment of you
I feel your flow to be true
Lifting my spirits on all that I be
It is of you that I can truly see
Whimsical, loving and confident to me
It is of us that I now see
Sitting together in this space that I call mine
Realising within of this time that is ours
Always of a knowing of you that I be
Beautiful within this that you be me.

The human form or eternalness that one is to see of themselves to be is always of a wanting of such to be more, this is to be the accepted understanding of this that you be. It is in the wanting of more that the tightness lingers within to stop the flow of such that we are to enter, for it becomes a belonging that you wish of self to have. To want of us is to be genuinely felt within your heart space to know of this that is to be ever destined upon your knowing of which it shall be.

The want comes out of the human characteristics of greed and impatience it is for us to witness to see. It is in this knowing that you could have, that one is to realise within oneself that it is in the doing of this that you need to be that one must release all ego and attempts at what you think it is that we be. For the shroud of secrecy is not of yours to realise, for it is of this that we are not, it is in the wonderful heart that speaks only to see love that is hers to be that the first glimpses will be seen of us.

Fear not to have not enough time within us, for your decisiveness to be this that we are is to be the door opener if to call it that, for this is where we shall start. We do not correct or criticize for it is of us that you are and in this it is that we trust. Your wanting of us is to be refined in a sensing of space that you call time, time as you see upon you planet is rushed, dreaded and often regretted, but to us it is limitless this space that we fill and all that is to become is for you. The initial offering in your space of reflections often fraught with dread of how to and what ifs it seems, this we are to offer that is how it shall go. Allow for all that is called forth to be in the correct space of this your time for all that you see is the unravelling of you that shall be.

We seek not of impatience from you within for this is the space that time does not appear in. Release all tensions that are of concern to be and it will slowly unfold for you to be held within this that we are. We sense the undoing of self as she thinks of this that is wrong within her, it is not of our doing that you are to change, it is in the becoming of this being in her time that she shall. No change is needed here from within for your inner knowledge of all that you have been is to allow for this understanding to impart your inner wisdom that is smart.

This wisdom we speak of has travelled many times over and over into this that we be the greater part of all that is to be seen as, the one, the true creator of the source and the ever knowing love that bounds all within it that is to be found within.

We seek of you to hear of this love that we be. It is in this understanding of this love to be that you will watch in contentment of this that grows ever so slowly daily and in time to your hearts opening in this space that is yours to be often found reminiscing of this to be true and sound within you.

Your wanting craves and carves a difference within you for you to see others that appear to be in a position of such that you are not, this appears to be so?

It is in this that one must know that all that is wanted is received in the time that it was scripted within to be for not all are forsaken if it is to appear that they are different to thee. It is in this that one must stand confident in her part of this that she be for the innerness that is you is in control of thee. She has spoken on your behalf many a times of this that you are and to receive of this is to be known to you in this that you have chosen of it to be. Release the desire to want more dear one for she is not of a hurry to be, she senses the urgency within the physical form to be insistent with each episode or quiet time to be done. It is in this urgency that one must wait trustingly for if you are not ready and this she will know it is not of your asking that it will be. All that is needed in this space that you call mine to sit is to be a resolution within oneself to partake in the timing of the universal laws of the flow of love and understanding of this that you shall be.

Your divineness grows within, it may start small this you need to know for it is attached to the bigger part that you already are to know. It is in this special place of connection to us that you will feel the real you begin to float. You are limitless it is to see here that all that you are to become you have already been.

> *We know of you well in this place that you now choose to sit, one of recognition as it begins to grow this relationship of you and me. For now, it is in your asking of us to be a wanting of more this we know and in this we ask of you to wait patiently as you sit here within us, is of you to grow.*

You speak of a wanting more why is this so?

The elation that you feel within oneself upon the discovery of us within is to be a feeling of such euphoria that it determines your success of us to be seen by you. Your earthly hearts become accustomed to the hardened form of such that one must at times intrust upon this that they be. But to feel of one's heart opening in such this space of love to be allows for this heart to see the world your place to live in a different view. A view that is tainted by love is such a knowing way of which it should be received. For this love is bold let us say in all that it is offering for you to sit into and once it hits you hard in the heart you will never need of another to be in this love that you think that they are of you to be. For all love is found within and it is the looking out to see this love in play that you will feel all distractions to go away.

You speak of this love openly as if it is to be the only love that one is to need?

We sense your needing of love to be proven amongst those of you that are to receive and offer this love to be. But it is often in this love that lays regret, grief, jealousy and hard work, let us correct you here. *YES,* this love that you experience in this time that be yours to experience brings much heart felt space of consideration to ones that are in the correctness of which it is to feel of this earthly love as it is known to you. And in this it is that we see the sensing of this love to be worthy of your attention and of a wanting of it to be. But to attach oneself to those of yours that you appear to love and respect is to always feel in a wanting of or a lacking of this love to be an option that is needed to be weighed up against one another as something of a self to be. It is in this human love that we see distraction to self to be for in the wanting of to offer this love to others often it leads to a lacking within self to be realised. So in this love that we speak of, the grandest love that is to be seen for it is the ruler of our universes this love that you are to see into, it has no limits, no asking of such to be for it sees all of you in such a way of perfection, that no giving of you is needed by thee.

Love upon this planet is very special to me. Are you saying that the love that I feel is not LOVE?

It is of this love that we speak with intention of it to be for in our realms of this love that we are there is no hesitation of such that you be. We see all that you are shining bright from within and in this true state that you be this is the love connection of all that be. We shine brightly through you to see so that all that you see are to feel of this love that you be and to know of this that we are to become of you to be. Your earthly love has it not come with trials and tribulations? Witness this yourself as you reflect into the loves that you have in this your now, or loves lost or wished of to be, this is the love that you were entitled to have for you have chosen all that is within you to offer to you this to know of love to be.

Growth comes out of the continual understanding of self and in this understanding of self grows a love that is willing to know of the all that you are to become.

It becomes bold and trusting within so that you need not doubt of self to be loved or able to offer and receive love. Seek not of this love to be yours to feel good about oneself for your true love, your true speaker is this that we be held tightly and ever so lovingly within you that you be.

CHAPTER 7

FINDING YOUR OWN TRUE LOVE

One must be allowing to find their own true love and let us offer for you to hear that your true love is different of that to another, for all true loves are to be accepted within self to be.

It is to feel many differences of this self to be, quieten the thoughts of such that you are, soften the voice in which it is that you speak, disregard that of another that is spoken out loud, see only of self to be, feel intention only from within, search not of another to be, seek only of love from within, for this is to be your path of self-discovery to begin.

Allow it to form out of itself this true and ever loving being of self, for the relationship that one is to have with self is to be allowed to develop into a loving yet at times it seems to be a challenging relationship to be said to offer. In the asking of this true love to come forth it will be challenged this we say in many ways, from physical speech, mind and emotions all attached to the human form that you be and commotion that is to be felt outside of this that you are to intercept within.

Feel as you grow adventurous with this that you are accepting of the smallest of challenges that are to appear in thought of this that you are. Feel as you allow the mind to wander away from you in a sense so that you can sit with no regret. It is of this offering here to you to say that the more time that you spend alone in this way the greater that you become. It is in this lonely space that it would feel to some that your truths are to become one and in the asking of you to see them for all that they be.

Out of this revealing of self to be true it is to be said by quite a few that this reveal within is confronting to see and often is contentious to the self to be seen. It will argue, this we know of your worth of this to be so, but be persistent in all that you do for the true knowing of you is to rise in her time it appears to be asked into and in this is the love that you are to seek. For in this love is us the true beings of light that we are. We will guide you into this place of service to be. It is not here, in the confusing thoughts of the knowing physical human mind that one is to want to listen intently, but from within, allowing of the eternal soul of you, that you are to hear of all that she has to speak for you to hear.

True love it is that we say is real, energising, refreshing, exhilarating to the old self to feel for it is not known to self to be of this state. It is to only feel of this love in a sense of not real to believe into this that you are allowing of it to be thought of as such that you be. No entitlements are given of right or wrongs of this love in the plainness of all that it be spoken in such a way that it is granted to every one of you upon your realisation of this form to be.

Sink into this love, let it swallow you as you are absorbed by it and watch as you change hesitantly at first, resisting to it we say, but the knowing of this that is to be felt will challenge all concepts of self-doubt within self. It is to be filled to your entirety of this essence that speaks of only the good that is to be held within all that we see. Be included in this moment of glee for the challenge that we see of the many of you to ask is in your ability to see that this is you and the glorious state of which it is that you can be.

Summon up the courage of this it is to ask for you are in this prime position of this to ask for. It is of this that is to be your now, this present moment of your time that you are to appear willing of such love to be understood and in this space of sense of worth and wanting to be, you will find the beautiful you within me.

It is in here that we stand confident, willing and sound to be true. It is of you that we are and in here it is to be said that it is of only you that we see. Stand into this asking of true love to be for it is yours to have and allow. We offer to you to understand what this true love is to be felt like within. It is to fill you to the brim of the further far reaches of yourself to be allowing not to be held within for it will seep this we are to say to all that shall come your way.

It is without resistance that one is to stand. For the ever-loving god that is to be found here in this spot is yours to stand into and feel of the whole that is to be the reasoning behind the feel of to want more.

There is no other that is to be found that can offer you this common ground with no competition with each other to compete for this place to be reached.

It is in your own accepting in this time that is you that you will want more of this self to be allowing of this completeness within to be felt.

Let go of the reins so to speak for it is in your guiding and justification of self to be that one is to hold to tight of this that you be. Limiting your beliefs of self to be, we seek not of you here in this space and find it hard to see of you in this limiting belief that you are to carry within.

In the releasing of all that you hold tight this intention within will speak with all her might, fear not of this voice not to hear, for she will guide you gently into this space. This space of willingness, this space of wanting, and this space of safe that you be, allowing of her you are to be.

We see only of this love that is true....

For you are always willing to return to this abundance that is I, and it is in the soul that she is to know of this that we are. Offering only this love that is true within us is it to be felt in the fullest upon your return.

We sit into the all that you are only in the asking of this to be, in the you that you are, you are all eternal within this that we see. It is only of the asking that you shall feel of our intention of self to be allowing of this true love to burst from within. For once it starts to transition, you will become a wanter naturally of more of this to show itself within you.

To start to see of this love within others is to feel the flow of intention as it should be, for it is not to hide this love from another it is our ask of it to be given in an openness of this love that it is.

For it is not of yours to hold within for we know it has been spoken to share of this love is sometimes to scare or intimidate, for the truth behind this love that is found is often hard to understand. It is to be said that many will not understand. In this we wish to say that this is okay. Their timing will be in the path of their own understanding of this love as it is to be found within them whether it be here in this that is now or later into another time of this that they are to discover. We sit intently within the many of you that are to witness of this love effortlessly yet continually exploring yourself to be. It is in the deepest of thoughts that you are to allow to exist that one will find truths that are yet to exist.

For in this space of recognition it is to grow deeply and ravishingly within, feeling the self-separate as such from the ever loving being of love that you are.

Do not feel disappointed of times when you are to sit in questioning of self to arise. The answers you seek are buried deeply within and are if allowed to become they all will be answered from this that you sit in. One must feel the trust within the self that she is to be this that you are to be allowed to become evident to the you that you are as the perfection that lays within.

It is in this way to think of yourself that one must....

It is often in thoughts such as these that you will feel the need to challenge the self as the owner of these thoughts and not the elite knowing within that is to speak of these images for you to receive. In the thinking self or the thinking mind it is to bring hurt and anger to the form that you are to feel as this is not of what it is that you are seeing into to be. The ego self and the forms natural way of which it has thought in this space of your life to be has never been challenged in this way before.

Allow for all anger, confusion and doubt to surpass, of this it will in time that you have.

It is a must to you to be in allowance of yourself to see through the intense knowing that is yours within, being ever guided by this that is love, to steer you into this place of recognition of yourself to be once again. We speak of this as a challenge in self to begin for it will feel like this in the first instance and the many that lay before you to interpret as yours to be.

In these challenges to be thought of as, is where the truth is to be found and it will lay itself out in the open for you to see the realness that you are.

Step into these thoughts of self to be and allow for all that you think of them to be not. It is in the disregard of self that these thoughts have come to be. In the many conflicts within self that these have become who you think that you are. It is never in love of spirit that one has allowed of herself to speak and in the love that you are searching for to be is the love that lays dormant yet ever knowing of self to begin to ask for her to rise. This she waits in a quiet determination of herself to be and in this she knows that the true love that you are will be felt , it will be remembered and it will become the very best part of you that you will interpret yourself to be. You will feel of this love as a completeness within you that allows you the impression of self to be satisfied and yet knowing of all that you are to become to be just as it will appear to you to be.

Seek not of this true love for it is of you this we know.

It is in the listening to self in varied moments of your days' time and energy that you possess here upon this lifetime that you will hear of the change to begin…….

Your physical ears are to become deaf to falseness that is spoken from this form and voices externally as they offer.

Your eyes become blind to the hardships and sadness and distrust that you see, for if the inner eyes are to look, it is in love that they will see. And in this looking of to be it is to feel of this that they are and know that they too are perfection in this that they are to be.

You will feel a sense of release to the way you once held things such as materials, possession's and offers of this to be, for it is in this love that is true that you will now know the true feeling of this that you are is everything to be.

Let this feeling wash over you for of this it is that you are complete in self and internal knowledge of this love that you are, always in-tune to the inner moments of self-doubt that may arise and in this we offer they do. See not of them as to be not needed for in growth comes much reflection of self to be and in these thoughts, you grow stronger in this voice that is to receive to speak of this that you are and all that you will be. Feel as you become adapt in self to acknowledge all that is to pass through you to think of, for this is the new you that is responding to the true voice of love that you have become.

To allow of self to think in this way you will find that each and everyday that you practise this within, you will feel more and more of the old self to depart this form that you are. And the changes that you notice, you will come to like very much and will find your voice of encouragement to become a willing supporter of yourself to be.

In this we offer to feel of this true love, one must practise patience, presence and peace in each and every moment of all your days that you are to offer this to your inner self to feel aligned within. For she knows not of any other way but these mentioned and it is in the learning of the physical to become a self-allowing student of this to be you a participant into, then you will feel this new journey of self to begin.

*In one's faithful agreement
to self to sit into this
timely practice in which
one must partake into,
it is in this space of
quietened mind to think
and release of all external
conformity to be, that
you will experience
into all these moments
as such of this that
you are to experience
as yours to be you.*

PATIENCE, PRESENCE AND *Peace*

"In these three words I choose to sit, in every moment of every day, so that I may feel ALL that is presented to me to see, to feel and to offer"

MY HEART FEELS FULL OF YOU.

*Your heart is full can you
not feel of it to be true?*

*Listen as you choose to quietly sit into
this space of respect and trust that you
have established within oneself to feel.
In the continual acceptance of self to be
perfection day by day, minute by minute,
moment by moment, word by word and
thought by thought in this process it is
to appear to you to think of yourself as.
One must be willing in all her truth's to
be heard, to be said, to speak of that you
are complete and loved by you and in
this acknowledgment of self to be. Watch
as you are to soar into this becoming of
the all that you are to be witness to.*

*It was out of true love
that you became,*

*it is into this true love
that you were born,*

and it is of this true love

*that you will become
once more.*

CHAPTER 8

INTERNAL CLEANSING

When one is to think of the self as to feel in need of a cleanse within, in this we are to notice that food, diet and the feelings of emotional attachments to self from within are to take the lead in thoughts of an internal cleansing to begin. This we must offer that in the thinking of self to need to lighten the offerings to be placed into oneself as in such of nourishment to be is the place that we witness most of you to start. For the intricate bodies of this form that you are designed of, with a presence in mind of this that we are to be seen into. It is in the intricate part of you that we speak of the internal systems digesting of foods that are continually offered to the system as in a need of support and a continual supplying of medicines and toxins that are to be integrated into the feeding regimes of the form to think of itself to need.

It is often this that is being digested within that one is to feel the need of self-sustainable thoughts of this that is to be a helping responsibility that one must undertake. It is to be said, the mechanics of the human form are in complete alignment internally within to the very essence of this that is the true speaker and interpreter of the knowledge that is needed for the human form to know of to nourish this body. And if allowing of one to hear, to feel, to respond to, it will be in exact correlation within oneself to be knowing of all that one is to require.

In the depths of the human mind to think of internal cleansing to be. We offer here to speak of that the initial thoughts that are attached to cleansing are initially the ideal response to mindful thinking of food. It is to be said here clearly that the first moments of thoughts to be of cleansing should be allowed to start with the physical mind and human emotions of thoughts of self to be.

It is in the allowing of oneself to think of themselves as a clear and intuitive vessel of love this is to be the hidden path of distraction that the many of you fail to allow oneself to venture along. In the seeing of self as a wanting of self to be received in a ever loving way to self and to all that you set your eyes upon then this is to be the first initial start that one should begin this internal cleansing with.

To first be allowing to see of self as a body of health and of an ability within self to heal by thoughts of self to be only of a perfection as such to be. Then one will start to feel the internal allowing of the words and conversations within self to take on a different approach to the usual that is offered in certain situations that one is faced with externally.

The knowing of self to be complete and of a true love recipient of the you that you are will determine the health of the external body to be. And it will allow for the eternalness that you are, to fill you with this love that can overtime generate a self-healing process that in time will prove to the onlooker that bides you to see that you are a worthy component of love that is to be felt.

In this offering it allows the internal knowing of you to offer to you the correct words and suggestions of this that you are to respond to. It is in this offering to self that you are perfect in all that you do. Human form is to think of perfection as such in the way as to which you think of it to be in the spoken word. Rethink these thoughts of the limitations that one is to put upon self to think perfection in the word to be spoken of as it is by you is to let one feel not of worth in comparison to be perfect compared to others. This is to be offered here that perfection is you in the all that you present for you are the only perfection that we see. Not of another that we must compare for you are the only light that we see to be you. It is of their own perfection that they be that we are to see them.

So, your perfection is just to be that.

Perfect for you.

This work is required by you to allow for all interpretations that are to come your way. Whether by self or others you are to override these comments, thoughts and feelings to be in the correct space of allowing, to feel of this internal you to be well.

To see self in a way of such love is to change the thinking first then the longing of self to be of another or something that they are not will shortly follow.

Must I then feel love for myself first?

To feel the flow of these kind loving words to enter your thoughts, mind and body is to begin the asking of more to be felt. It is in this space that one is to ask of that we are to witness the insistent need for the body to require attention to thinking of itself to be a body of love rather than not. For here in these words of love that one is learning to speak to self and to others one will find the need to allow for the body to respond to the extra attention that it feels alignment with. It feels the need to communicate to you the thinker of self to be this insistent want of the body to feel clear and satisfied with nourishment that is to help calm, nourish, reduce inflammation and fuel the body in a sense of to be fulfilled from within. In this searching of to be fed initially the human form is to go to great lengths to diet and seek the advice of others to implement a certain type of eating/foods or supplements to suit of what it is that they are looking for. It is here that we are to offer that your inner being of love that she is, is to be the greatest teacher here in this your now of all that you are to seek help into. She is the knower of you that you are and of what it is that you need. If one is to allow the body to speak it will in feelings, sensations and movement of such the inner knower of you to be will help guide you to the correct nourishment of internal needing that is wanted. It is in this that one is to seek externally looking for the correct formatting of nourishment to be. It is to be said here that your bodies are to know of this that they are needing. And your body will feel the urge once the mind and the speaker feels clearer to interpret of this language of love that is spoken gently to self. So, that she will feel responsive to the asking's from within as to what it is that you are now to crave internally. Hidden by the attraction of much that is to be offered here upon this earthly planet to the human form as such in the deliciousness of the foods that are to be delectable to the palate of the beholder to taste. It gets tricky here this we are to offer. For you as tasters of these types of foods over such a long period of time have become addicted to thoughts of these foods to represent a certain type of feeling, emotion or longing attached to these to be ever presented to you in your daily intake of them. It is in this that we offer to you that the initial changes mentioned above in regards to self-speak and the willingness to listen to the inner voice of love first that is to represent you in all this love that you be, that you will feel the certain urges attached to these foods begin to diminish. This will allow clarity in thought of these foods that are to be a new requiring for you to be allowed to enter your thoughts in such a way as to be the nourishment that you are in want of.

When one is to feel the need to self-love and be attracted to the inner voice that speaks so lovingly of you, it is not of a wanting from the external realms that you sit into that one is to seek of a gratification of self to be. The need then to supplement oneself with foods that are no longer to feel as needed by this human form ceases to exist.

One will find the attraction to the foods that generate health in a natural way of which it is that they are presented. You will fill the void that once was filled by thoughts of materialistic objects to desire, others and the need to respond to these others to be a worthiness in self to be.

It is to be said here that all foods become alive within themselves to become and it is the foods that are naturally giving of life to ones that are to eat of these foods that you will soon feel the feelings of health and sustainability grow within. It is to be said that no food is to appear to be off limits for you are all in your own knowing of self to choose as you so desire of them to eat. But we will offer here to you to know of, that the certain types of foods that are to soon become your first choice to choose will suggest to you a sense of life and longevity to become yours upon their consumption. These foods will speak to you in a way that you are to resonate with and the internal craving of the body's response to them will allow for the feelings of the need to internally cleanse within to become apparent within you.

It is the mind that is to control the thoughts of foods to be of what it is that appears to be a wanting by the human that holds this mind in thoughts of self to be. It is the reluctance in self to give up these foods for the love of a product or food to be. We offer no suggestion to you as such as to what it is to consume, for to try and change these choosing's within self-becomes apparent as the mind is to wander into the regions of this is something of a wanting it needs. Here we offer that it is to have become an addiction to the substance or product that you are choosing to partake into.

The human body interprets itself so often by what it is that it feels it is needing in this time of need to be asking of it to be felt within. So, it is in this journey that one is to feel the need for the internal cleansing to begin, that one will feel the releasing within self of thoughts around substance, foods and emotions of these to be attracted to. This will ease the thinking mind so that the inner voice can speak and be heard clearly.

It is to be in the appearance of self that you will rise into, for the self is to respond to the words or encouragement and love that you speak. It is in this form of all originality that you exist as chosen by you to be, that you won't feel the need to be of another. It is to see of oneself as the only you that is to be and that you will find this chosen path within to become once more of the ever-guided soul that you are to be.

We love the originality that you all bring and it is to be said here that in respect for oneself in regards to the loving being that you are, all good things of the highest of intentions shall follow and become an ever knowing within self of this beautiful being that you are. It is in this that our intentions are to be spoken of here to receive as advice to those of you that are still in self-doubt of all of this that you are to become.

Let us speak to offer that this does not come easy to the human form, for much water has been allowed to flow under the bridge so to speak and in here to hear of the truth that you are is the hardest place to sit. You are to erase the feelings of neglect and criticism that still linger here, for you have experienced all of these, Is this not correct?

You are to know of the feelings that these reactions have attached themselves to you as, Is this not correct? You know of what it is to feel as not enough, Is this not correct? You are to feel the need to want to be you in this space of love once more, Is this not correct?

We see you all as you stand there in your rawness that this chapter may encourage you to feel within, for it is in the hidden sadness within that the many of you are still to hold that you feel this need to disagree with the loving voice of intentional love within. Let her speak of this we ask for she is your true guider of this ever-embracing true love that you are to be. Resist the urge to disagree for it will serve you no good to self to be, and we offer here that the smallest of intentions within are to be the most accomplished parts to begin the changes within that we are to see. Feel the loving space needed for you to allow for this chapter to resonate within.

It is in this space that you are to sit that if you feel the need to rest and release of all that you be, we offer this to you.

In the becoming of all that you are to be one must be of a wanting and in allowing of the true self to be seen. She is to have been hidden by this physical beast that you be and she has been quietly sitting within you this form that you are, waiting patiently for this moment to arrive. This she knows to speak of you in great truth that all that you be is to be the beautiful you that you have always been.

Becoming of you this love is to be felt, for you are of this love intentionally to be felt. And in this love, it is that we sit patient, knowing and supporting of you to always be. We will be all that you ask of us to be and in this we speak of truth, love and compassion of the gracious you that you be for us to see.

ALLOWING TIME FOR YOU TO SIT INTO………

Here we offer to you to know to receive in the hearing of this you will feel complete to ask the questions that this chapter was to bring forth into your asking of to be. WE ask that you feel of self to want to sit and just be. Here in this that you are you have no place to be, no other to speak of and no one to be. WE feel your tenderness and trepidation of self to be wanting of this to become, for it is to be said that those of you that are to choose of this place to sit into, your old self will never want to come with you it would appear to you to be seen. Feel as the place of resistant self is to arise, for she knows not to what it is that is to hide inside. This place we encourage of you to sit is your place of contentment and quiet that is to speak the deepest of knowing's to you to hear. You have not forgotten of this we speak for it is just buried deep into oneself so that it needs to be released to be heard. In her you will hear of all the great that you be.

Sit quiet in your time and let all that is to surface to feel and be said, it is safe in this space that you have chosen to sit. We receive all that you think and offer a kind knowing of this that you be. You will feel the urge to resist this feeling of place to sit for you are used to being busy in thought of self to be and do. It is in here that one must be patient to self and allowing of this space to connect. It is of great love that you will find in the wandering eye and the inner mind of us to be. We see only of you in this space of love to be and in this wanting of yours to ask of it to arise it shall be felt in your entirety of you to be. It is only of this space that is to be yours to be felt for no other is to offer this for you to sit into. It is only of you this peaceful being of this that you are that you will release all of what is not of a wanting in no terms of its harshness to be. Let all that is needed to be spoken here in this space feel able to be said, we are not to judge this of you to be speaking within. For your words will soon change this we are to know. In this offering of space for you to take refuge into this you will experience one to be of growth, nourishment, calm and safety to be. It is of us and not another that you are to suggest this space to be, for you are the only willing component that we are to see. This is yours to feel into and sit intentionally within. Here it is that you grow from within as the external that you be will slowly slip away, but to be patient of this we are to say. You are to know of all that is to be correct in all that you see as your story that is unfolding of you to be within. We seek not of reverence or a promise from you, for you are free to come and go as you please, let us just say to be wise, that if you spend your time within here in this space that is yours to create that you will get to become the greater being of love that you are intended always to be. No limits to time or suggestions are to be placed for you will feel the need as to how it is to be within to be felt in here to be of your own knowing as such to be. Seek not out of ego that you must be here, for you are to be always of a wanting of this to be. It is to grow within you this place of self-respect for in here it is that all that you see will be considered into a different sensing of themselves to be.

Cleansing of such to be is to view of self to be the inhibitor of this form that you are to present to one another in your appearance of self to be. It is in the depths of the reality that is to exist within that one must feel the need for this internal cleansing to take place. Watch as you grow in all aspects of self to be releasing of the old, the heavy and the regret that one has carried for self to be in this lifetime so to pass. It is in the internal dialogue that the cleanse is to begin for here in this form the heart is the seer of this that we are and is to be the hearer of all that is to be in need of to be spoken out loud for ones such as yourselves to hear. We are the bearers of this love it appears and in this love that we present to you upon your willingness to feel of the internal cleanse within allows for the wraps and covers of all that you have hidden beneath to be revealed and allowing of this light to be felt.

The cleansing process is not only of the physical form to be felt but is very intensely attached to the soul that is to strive within. For she to remembers upon her entering of this life to be that she was once and knows of this to be again that she is to be the internally cleansed being of the light, love and compassion of all that is to be.

The thought of an internal cleanse is a response to self to want to feel the change of direction within one from the neglected, forgotten self to be heard to become the evanescent being of love that she is always to be. Feel as this body, this form is to shed the outer layers of time that have been allowed to be dumped upon her. For it is to be spoken that mostly if not all of you are to carry these as burdens to be and the need to be heard once more to hear of this forgotten voice of love that is you.

You will feel the insistent pull towards the rewiring to understanding of self to be, feel the freedom to stand into oneself once more.

Pure, loved and full in the ability to be this that you are without constraints placed upon oneself as to search in another of this to be said to hear. It is not of this that you will be needing in the choice that you are willing to make that all that you are is the us that we be.

I feel that there are many that offer their way to me as a "How to guide to interpret", shall I allow this to be?

We sense of this to be a knowing within yourselves to be and it is in the excitement to find of this knowing within to begin one must feel the urge to spread the word to speak of this that we are and the place into which one is to sit. If one is to be allowing of this to be information as to the speaker to be theirs then you will not feel the need to listen to it as your own knowing of it to be. Let it all flow forth for in their truth it is theirs to know and it is in your place of which to receive that yours is to be allowing to be seen. We offer this to the many that have searched to find this exquisite place to be thine within and it is to become a reality all of their own that they must resonate into. For no one is able to place this space of love into you, for you see it is already there to begin. It is the human form that must be willing of this to be found and this she will in her time of which it was to be offered to her to begin. So, listen not too hard to news from another. It is of the curious mind that one is to listen to find that one will seek the words to be spoken to find this within themselves to be the same as spoken of. It is in the reality that is yours to be that you will find your own way and the less that you are to interpret to receive from another the truer your journey of self will be. Reunited you will be of this we are to offer of the being of love that you are sustained within to belong eternally. And in this it will be your sense of knowing her so well that the words of another will not ever replace those that you hear yourself to speak.

Imparting this knowledge for me to hear....

You shall clearly in one's decision to be heard from within, in this hearing of self to be the thoughts that you are of this with intention of all that she shall be. Know it is to allow for the new found knowing that is to grow within to expand all thoughts of this that you are and to allow for the out reaches of yourself to extend to all that you are to witness into this life that you are. WE see of this growth to be allowing of such to hear all that she is needing of which it is to hear. But one must be willing to listen to the voice that is to speak the clearest and with such divine intention and devotion to you to hear of. For this voice that is to fill you will follow your every command it is this that you are to know, so choose wisely of your words to speak so that you will not feel the need to repeat the past that has hung off you like distress into this that you have allowed yourself to become. It is in this loving voice that you will feel complete, sit intentionally into her voice and hear of the whispers as they grow to the extremeness of this that you are to be.

IN ONE'S GROWTH WE SEE,

We are to honour all that you are here in this space with much respect for yourselves as you are to willingly sit into this expansion that you are. Allow for the growing within to begin so that one may feel of this insistent need to cleanse to be allowed to be seen in the true eyes of the hidden beholder of the real reasoning into why it is that one is to feel incomplete in all that she is to see, eat and be.

Willing it is that you must be to forsake all that you think of this to be the cure for the inner gnawing of this that you fight with. Be allowing of the real you, the proud you, the prominent you, the ravishing you and most importantly the loving you to be seen in all her glory as the one that knows the correct conversations of word for you to partake into. Be allowing of her to guide you as we are, to see you become the controller of this wisdom that is yours to hold into as the ever knowing divineness that you are of.

CHAPTER 9

FEELING THY HEART

My heart speaks loudly of this I know. It is in the wanting of it to be heard that I do. The heart that we think of it to be is to be the most extravagant piece of you in this human form that you are. It will never steer you wrong or speak of untruths in the enabling of self to listen to its loving words that it will speak. This heart space that is to be contagious we offer to the believer once it is felt, for in here it is that the earthly love that you sit into is to first respond to thoughts of those that you are to be fond of. In here it is the heart that speaks wisely of this that you are to feel. The transitioning from the feeling heart space to a quick to think thought is what will overrule the heart, the thinkers mind is to be the conqueror we speak of this to be so. Let all that flows firstly from within this heart space that is to be known as the love centre of the body, the communicator of this pure first felt love to be is to be the speaker that one is to crave to hear in each and every time that she is to speak. Your hearts we see are to be filled with many stories of told and regrets to have lived, it is filled to the brim with spaces of nonchalant and lovers to have been. The needs, wants, desires and asking's of self and for others live in this space, this we know. Your heart in this form that it is to be is to be able to commence within itself this knowing of all that you be, for it is to feel intimately this that you are and in here it is that your love for oneself is to be found.

This heart of yours feels so unable at times to be accepting of this voice to speak within of this love that you be, she seeks refuge in your human thoughts of not to be. The heart and mind are not trusting friends you know for the mind is to challenge of all that she is to see to be felt, revisiting scenarios of late to be told to her to hear of over and over again in this life and those that have been reviewed. She struggles with the strength of this mindless giant to be, for although smart in need of to be in the human form to connect into all that she is to be physically, it is the mind that will challenge self-thoughts of you to become complete once again.

Watch as she seeks refuge within this thinking space to be overlooking the heart that sits patiently, lovingly from within wanting of this to be seen, holding this god that is to sit deep within. She is to know that once contact is to begin you will not follow your thoughts of this you think you to be but be in full allowance of this great space within to rule you to your days that are to end.

Your heart is filled with endless magic, and in this form that you be, one must sit still in patience so that this heart may speak to guide you in your language of love that you are in a wanting of which it is to hear. For no other heart space can or will speak like yours this is to be the loving voice that is only for you to hear. Determination within self must prevail for the heart is conscious of this that you are in the we that we be. So, feel as she wants you to understand that the many thoughts that are yours to experience are often of no use to you to be. In a glance of self through the eyes of the heart, one will if not accustomed to this view will hardly recognise this to be you. She sees only of a complete love to be seen and in this trusting soul that is you, you will face many thoughts of this not to be the face that you see to be you. We see not of you standing there in this form that you be but only of the light that streams from this heart that we know. We feel all intentions good and bad that you allow to flow through this space to be yours, it is in the changing of self from mind thought to heart felt that this space will open to appear to you as the right timing of yourself to allow and entertain these thoughts of you to appear.

Your earthly heart spills over with this physical love that you feel and yet it also holds onto those that have ceased to be and left you alone. This feeling space within is to be the centre of all that you be, we feel it as it speaks to us in the knowingness of this that we are to interpret all that you silently speak.

Your body's heart is willing to be in this place if only you can allow your thoughts to be not of us to be a wanting but a knowing from within to be.

We see every one of you to travel into this time to be yours, to ask of us to keep reminding you to be the ever knower of this that you are. So that your need of others to fill your heart becomes not, but only your true words that you speak lovingly of self to be. Watch as this space grows into a trusting and knowing connection that be only of you. For all that see in this the revealing of it to be shown, will only want to know more of why this is to be this that you are to feel so comfortable once more within your own skin and want it for their own.

Know this heart that is to speak, is far wiser than you have ever imagined it to do, once you feel the vibration that it is to make, let it speak easily of this love and the way it is for you to go. You are to seek directions this we know from others that are to surround you in this life, yet it is not of your heart that they are to speak. Kind and caring words yes, they may be, but not the words that you are needing to hear.

My heart feels heavy with all that it carries. How do I allow for it to open?

One must be pleasing to self in speech and thoughts to be. For it is of this that you will feel the slightest of urges develop within that will be allowing of you to connect into this space that you call your heart. This heart was never designed to carry the burdens that you do, it was to be the life centre of you in this form that you be only to do its job as such. It is in the human way that you have struck a chord with this life to be felt. That ones such as you have taken upon your own will to carry of these thought's and distrust of this that you must to punish self or cherish those that you hold dear to you to feel.

 Know of this, that this magical space universally loved is only to hold love in this that you be in a connection to us. So in here we ask of you to be smart and allow for all that does not sit lovingly within, is to be offered here in this exact moment of your now to those of us that find you to be in this space of connection within us. We are many that see into this space, and in here it is that we are to exist willingly asked by you to be. This physical heart it appears is to hold desperately to all that appears to be offered for ones such as you to see. Let the need to hold whether good or bad, be freed from thoughts in this sensing of self to be needing and it will open up space in great proportion. So, that the need to exist in this space called thought within will no longer be a need by you to feel into.

When the heart is allowed to speak and you find her voice to be complete, you will endeavour in all your days that are to remain to become the wanted listener to all that she speaks. Her words will never change of this we say for she speaks of the wisdom that lays deep within the ALL we know. It is in this way of which it is that she speaks that all your dreams of you to become are to exist.

MY HEART FEELS SWOLLEN, DOES YOURS?

Writers interpretation of her heart to feel.

In my allowing of this my heart to be heard it felt strange to say the least, for I was not yet fully in a space to allow for myself to hear clearly of all that was to be said, as I bet you are to be the same. To feel the releasing into something that was not to be seen. It was in here that I felt this love of myself to grow to the wanting of this to be seen by myself more and more in each allowing of my space to be. In this space that I speak is my time of peace and calm that I have become accustomed with to be allowing of self to be. I now want for this time to be free to wander amongst those of you that are to guide me eternally and of you that I am. It is in this knowing that my heart feels full to the brim. It is to hurt at times I am to say for the love that I feel in this way wasn't always easy for me to feel, and it has become as it will in you a trusting voice and way to feel.

Letting go of myself the physical form and inviting the light in here in this space, that is to become for all that seek of it to. You will find as I did the need for less to be said and the want of no more to be received externally. For it is of in here that I speak the outer limits of which you are to reach you will feel the love to be so bold in its feels, that no one or other place is quite the equal to this that I now call mine as I sit contentedly within. I watch with love in every day this that I am to become for I have opened my heart to this bigness in every way and it is of these words that I wish to say. In here I am love and it is of this love that I feel in all that I do in everyday that I see. This swollen heart of mine offers me guidance in all that I do, and it helps guide me in just this that I be ever knowing of this love that I see. It is to be allowing of me to be the seeing eyes that I see all of you.

This love isn't always easy they say......

This we agree for to come out of humble thoughts it will feel as though it is not of yours to be. It will detour you into thoughts that you are to be. Speak openly of this love in this that you are to write, to speak for it is a challenge that one will feel like they need to compete. It is of others that will appear to have all of this in hand. You this we say, must not be deterred for in every moment of your heart that you feel it will tell you of what it is that does not feel to be yours. To view of self is all that you will need to do, to watch as this task or chore that you see it to be at times, become easier for you to do. Retrace your steps of self to be and allow for kind thoughts into this that you now are to know that all that you spoke or felt was out of the need of which you did not know. You are wisdom from within and it is to be said that in the speaking of your words you will grow bigger within this space to connect and in here it is that you will be capable to quickly correct of what it was said that you are to regret. The reversal of hurting words is in your wanting to be, Is it not? We offer you here that in your thoughts of self to grow wise into this that you are to become that you will falter in thoughts of another to speak if not just and simply to be loving in all that you say.

This we offer gets better each day in your knowing power that lays within. You will feel the need less to offer your thoughts and opinions upon another and watch as they are to grow under the loving gaze that you are to develop yourself to become of.

If one is to start with this one simple question, ASK....

"HOW DOES MY HEART FEEL TODAY?"

Write upon these pages the feelings that you are to feel in one's own heart today. It is of you to allow for all that you feel within this heart of yours to speak whether it be full, laden, weary, saddened, brave, trusting or loving. Be truthful in your writings as you record of how it is that one's heart is to feel over the passing days. Notice what is stirring within as you read these pages of script. Let surface what may, so that you can with intention feel free to record thoughts, feelings and moments that may be needing to be heard.

....
....
....
....
....
....
....
....
....
....

Your words that are written; of this we are to feel reign supreme within all that you are to know. For in the heart that is you she will find courage for you. The external battles of form to be wanting of this that you're not will surely make this journaling hard to begin. Seek not to feel self-conscious of all that you choose to write for it is the real you that we wish to hear, and not of the ego's thoughts into how it should appear. The writing that is yours if you let it flow, will become soothing to some, for others it will be angry words upon paper that you wish to show, tears of joy or happiness will show themselves in a wanting to become. In the writing that you do we hear of all that you wish to be spoken of in this way to release. Pen to paper is to write, for in your heart she helps to offer all that is correct of this your time to free your thoughts from the barrage of mistrust so that you may feel of us. Supporting and guiding you in this place of offering in all that you feel the need to dislodge from that heart space within.

Allowing your words to flow………

It is to feel the flow of all that one is to know of the true existence that is to dwell within. For it is in this knowing that you shall be the holder of all that is to exist within this that we are. To allow oneself to flourish under the pretence of what it is not to be felt by yourself, is to surely be misleading into the direction of which is not yours to follow. But to be allowing and sitting in the receiving of this that you are to be into of this magnificent beauty to be you. Then this is to be correct and the ever-knowing path of your so choosing to become.

One's only path or guidance as you would write it to be heard by you, is to feel of this direction of which it is to appear that one is to follow. But let us offer to you to hear that all directions are known by you to be in your so choosing of them to be and it is not of a single path that you are to follow onto for all paths are wide in presentation of them to see.

It is in all that is within and to surround you, that are in the ever knowing of all that is to flow into you to be in receiving of all directions as yours to view into as the correct position to enable your hearing of the best direction that is being guided to you.

We see of your asking of this change to be felt within your thoughts of what it is that you are to think yourself to be worthy of, to have, for it feels to be an internal battle of what is to be thought of as a waste of your time. Allow yourself to feel freely in all that you deserve. One must adjust their thoughts and speaking that surrounds of all that you do to think and say for it is in this that the greatest changes are to become apparent to oneself and to those that are to surround you in your viewing of this to be.

It becomes a knowing within this way to feel of this that you are wanting, does it not?

For all that are to witness this phenomenon is to be in awe of such that it is to appear, no restraints or restrictions upon what is and what isn't. It is in the feeling of emotional attachments to such beliefs that determine your thoughts into this that you do not have or not believe yourself to be.

If in this very instance if you were to think of this to know, that all that you are wanting is yours to be.

Allow for yourself to sit into this knowing of this that is all the same.

It is to offer no resistance in intensity to you or another it is simply the thoughts of the human mind that the non-allowing or negative thoughts are to occur.

Think here of all that you have written and reread with love in your heart. Offer yourself forgiveness to the words that appear upon your pages if they feel hurt, saddened, not spoken or simply forgotten.

Let yourself be full of love for this being that you are and start here to say that;

I am worthy of all that is to be mine, for I am no different in this that is to be .For I am of this loving, infinite energy that is to rule the worlds that are to be of the one true presence within all that is. So, it is of my choosing to know of this to feel into that I am worthy of all that I ask to be?

Thankyou

CHAPTER 10

I LOOK TO SEE

You all falter in this space of time to be at times to see the real self to be. Feel into this space that we are to offer here for you to be, that it is only of you that we ask to see. Not of another one must present, for it is not of them that we are wishing to see. Look deep within as the feelings are to grow and the confidence of this that you are is to become.

To take the leap of faith it is to be heard that the so many of you are to do, for in here that it is to appear that we are, is your willingness to hear of this that we speak. Let us offer to you to know that there is no in here for you to go. Looking internally is correct and you will find the times that you're to reflect of self to be leading you inwardly rather than away from this that you be. Feel not to lose control, for you are the commander of this ship and it is of you that is to be heard in the wanting of us to become knowingly and willingly once more into your thoughts of us to be, so that your heart is to feel of the need to be. Reminiscing you will become of all that is to be seen, for in your thoughts that are to be guided now by the heart that you are allowing of which to hear is the remembering of this way of life to be. You've seeked into many this we know, and it is always in a wanting of you to grow.

Here in this now your soul is to soar for she has been present in all that you've become and is to be the leading hand in to which it is to learn here upon this to be your planet to live upon.

She beams at us can you not yet see. It is her radiance of self that we see, for in her trueness of such it is just her that we see.

BE allowing of this form that you are to witness the being within for she has been waiting to see this that you are reflected from the mirror that you hold up to see oneself within. Let us offer to you now that the changes aren't fully complete for one is to work deeply in to begin this massive feat. The work begins in this place that you first stood begging, pleading and asking us if you should.

WE are pleased that you did for the original version of you that is to become is the remarkable work that we see presented to us. We watch as your confidence grows this wanting of such to be able to take more than a peek of the new self to be. Trading woes and worries for true love and courage is the role that you must take for you are in this wanting to be this we promised to you to keep.   To see out of your eyes to watch as this miracle that you are is to take her first step into what is to be known as the eternalness' that you are to sow, showering others with this new love for self to be found.

With lessons a plenty for you to learn and in this hurriedness that one is to feel complete, we ask of you this to enjoy every splendid moment that is to exist. For you are always in our eyes as this vision to see and to feel of you in connection with thy is to be the most rewarding joy for us to intercept.

WE see of you standing here in this that you thought of your self never to be, allowing and loving in all that you do, craving the want of this to be more within you. We speak of this want to be more as in an extravagant way, for it is to be felt a need within that is to haunt those of you that are too quick to wish this space to allow for more of this to be filled in. We are not to be concerned by your time for it is in this that you asked to begin, you are to be reminded in all of each timing that you are to become coherent within, and allowing of the searching to begin. It is of us to say here that you are never lost but simply have learnt to misplace this love that is yours to now see again in the innerness eye that you have become. You are to be revealed to self this pleasant sight to see it is one of truth and just that you be. The want to be more is obvious within and in this one must keep the quest alive so that all that you are to seek will unravel inside. It is in the wanting of this that we are that you feel the reminiscing of this that we be. We have loved you from afar it would seem. But in the new learnings of how to be once more in our channels of which sits love you will feel that we aren't as far away as you thought. And in this you start to trust yourself to speak to us willingly and asking us to become an ever prominent source of this that we are to be within once more.

Each day you are to undertake as the newest start within for you will not be in need to see of the old self again. She will reveal her wants and concerns of this we are to know. In this strength of yours that is now love within being heard in all her glory to be you will hear her to speak in a new way shall we say often covered up by your response in a loving way. Gentle to her you will be for she will feel fragile and lost in her sense of self to be for she has been this to you in this way for a long time.

It appears now that you can see her in the clearing of such the heavy haze that you thought of yourself to live into has disappeared. In just this one asking to be, you were heard in a clear and trusting way from us to be you again in the feeling of self to be recognised so that all that you came here to be is to open up for you in this new willingness that you have yearned.

I often get asked this by my guides in the voices of love that I hear....

WHAT IS IT THAT YOU ARE WANTING?

At first, I was unable to answer for it felt to me to be not of a wanting of self to be. I felt guilty shall I say to be asking of such them to be in any way that would make me feel as to benefit from. I soon learnt with their persistence that they showed in the continual asking of me to answer them in a certain way. That it was of them to speak to me that I hear clearly channelled through this form that I am. That I was to ask of them in all that I was wanting of to know and it is to have been felt within this soul that I am that she was to connect in such this beautiful way. That my voice was to become theirs so that I may understand all that I hear of them to speak.

In their love I grow more and more connected in every way for it is of them that I am and in them that I request to stay. It is of no doubt this they are to say "the all that are to ask of us in this way shall be heard to speak with the internal being within". In this I soon learnt that I was no different from all of those that are still to hear their own unique voice of spirit to be guiding and loving of them in this way.

For you see when it was to first become apparent that I had a voice in my head I struggled to hear it clearly and to understand of what it was to say. I soon learnt with their guidance every day in which it is that I still sit in, this voice is mine, travelling within me from the destiny of the many that I have become in the knowing space that I now call love. Our universe it seems is to be big to comprehend but this I have seen to be even more than the extreme thought of it to be. So in here it is that I sit willing and in full acceptance of self to be wanting the more that I am asking of to be. Watching from afar it was that I thought of them to see me to grow internally and eternally the "I Am" that I am to be once more. This I soon discovered that I was to be not as far away from them as I thought, for it has been spoken to me in many times that we've spoke, that they are the ones that are to sit within this me that I be so that I can sit in them to be.

I look forward to the day when my journey here is to be complete, not to hurry it to be, for I am often told to be present in all that I do here for it was of my asking as such. But in a trusting knowing of my death it shall be my choosing of it to be a wanting in the most extravagant space of it to become. And I shall meet again the loves of my life, they will know of my return for in this instant passing to the space to recollect and review.

I am absolutely sure that all that I have heard to speak with will embrace me fully into this space of unconditional love upon my return once more, ready to cherish all that I am in this that I am to bring to them to see. It is of them that I choose to sit into every day for it is of them that I feel in my heart space to know of in such an intense way. This in them I do trust for they are friends to be and in this I ask of them to remain still within me offering up all that they are to help me to receive. I want of them in this life that I am to be for I will not ask of them not to be.

In the ease to listen that one is to do your readiness will appear as mine did too. I asked of them to be known to me and in my heart of love it was to appear these voices of spirit that now I hear and love.

Always grateful in love that I am to receive.

CHAPTER 11

BOLD IS YOUR COLOUR

Be bold in all that you are to sit. Not of the ego we speak to become, for in this sensing of self to be strong one must override the inhibitions that one is to feel in the sensing of self to feel real. You are exquisite in the sensing of this to be found within all that are asking of it to be. You see yourself surrounded by things that cannot be done and in your voice that is weak we hear uncertainty. It is not of this creature to be in thought of all that you cannot be. Your boldness develops from within carrying with it a subject such as thee. You are to be willing in yourself to want of this directness that is to make way for the voice that is yours to find its volume in which it will speak.

> *To be of this boldness is to see self and all that you are as whole and complete.*

One is not to offer this to another in a confidence that you will feel growing from deep within. This is only yours to feel, no one needs to know of this talk that you control in yourself to hear, let it guide you away from the everyday thoughts of self to be unseen, unheard and unwilling to participate into. For it is of you that we see glowing brightly in the magnificent hue that you project from within. This is the new colour that you crave, and in your acceptance, it shows yourself in the boldness that you are meant to be.

Becoming bold is to feel no concern or thoughts of others to allow. The many feelings and thoughts of such that seemed important once upon a time are no longer. You feel the difference in your stance of this that you are, for you feel as though you can do no wrong. You start to hear all that is to be corrected within one's head, in the knowing of source that is there to speak instead.

In this newfound boldness you appear different to feel, different to see. In a wanting of this confidence that you will find and the braver you become, the bolder you be.

Can we ask you to be Bold in your asking of this that we are to be?

Can we ask you to be Bold in your thoughts that all is as it should be?

Can we ask you to be Bold in your thoughts of you to see?

Can we ask you to be Bold in the knowing of this that is?

Can we ask you to be Bold in the willingness that you are to want?

Can we ask you to be Bold in your surrender to the All that be?

Can we ask you to be Bold in your voice that you are to speak?

This we offer, You may not yet be able to answer a yes or even contemplate a thought as such to be yours to feel as though you may ever be willing or ready to read these statements that are offered to you by us. In us it is to offer to those that are willing to open their hearts and use these words as a guiding path to your understanding into this that you are to be.

Feeling bold needs not to overwhelm, for in the asking of self to allow for this boldness to set in, know that it will self-correct. If you are to neglect love and let the ego have its way and without a doubt it will try and sway you into the mind that thinks of bold to be big, loud and showy. "See me in this way "it will say. You will feel the need to self-evaluate in this life as situations arise, for the knowing of self in a boldness that shines compared to a boldness that is to be despised will emerge to your knowing of this that you are and will not want to be. You'll be quickly reminded that when you choose of boldness that is to shine rather than boom, then you are to hear of your heart to speak, only kind ambitions for self and all that you are to know.

Boldness that we offer to suggest is not attached to the human ego in the sense that you think it should be. In boldness of character and the wanting of us to be ever present within self once more becomes a confidence and satisfaction of self to see.

The sensing of a feeling of strength that is to grow from within, one must never confuse this sensing of self to be bold in a form that is to arouse others with the demands that a bold scenario can encourage.

It is in this form of boldness that one is to discourage the thoughts of themselves to be, for the so called bold meaning upon your planet will entice a different reaction from your innerness to be the offering to you, the true meaning that you think of it to be.

It is in the inner knowing of self that the bold being of love that you are to beckon forth from within once more, knows to wait patiently observing of this love and watches it grow into this connection of yourself with source, spirit, god, and the all-knowing love that we exist into. And it is in here that your boldness of yourself becomes eager and aware of you to find yourself again confident and willing to stand to view of all that you are destined to know.

Be BOLD in your asking of us to BE.

To be bold takes courage in the allowing of one to unburden their thoughts of themselves to be not. You are this rare creature that has developed an opinion upon self and all that you are to see.   Fore go these thoughts as such of self, for this is of what this world is to need, more of you that are making a promise with yourself to allow of your boldness to beam. Expressing from within this beautiful you that you be.

The sensing of others in this miraculous state when viewed from your aspect that only sees love is to cherish oneself and grow from all that they see upon another's commitment to themselves to be brave enough to say,

"Today, I choose BOLD".

Keep it hidden if you must, for it is only of you that needs to know. Have no need to speak of it to be. Trust only in you. We need no reminding of this bold that you are. Our intentions are only of this love to be felt within you that you are to become bold in your own right of all that you are.

Watch as this newfound boldness fills your physical form encouraging and accepting of all that you want to see. Fight not with this determined form, for she now has an innate ability from within to see how her adventure is to become. Guided and steered with the directions of bold talk from this that you have allowed to transform within. Listen as she speaks, this your heavenly inner voice that reassures with a certain knowing of this that you were destined to be.

To be bold is to be direct in the sensing of self to be and it is to be said that in your asking of self to be, it is to want of this boldness to be heard, for in this it's never misunderstood. Ask of us to be bold in all that you do, never to be mistaken in a voice that is not heard. In you it is that you stand bold, loud and proud of who it is that you have become for it was in the boldness that you asked many times ago to be of this person that is willing to speak in the ever knowing of all that she is and in what she is to become.

Your voices have become distant in self to hear, we offer to know.

Allowing of this to become commonplace within this form of the indecisions to be, one is to witness uncertainty and forgets of this knowing surge from within that all that you express is correct and right to be yours in your understanding of self to hear.

In love and a willingness to be this, is what is needed. Bold in this way is not to be worn like a badge, garment or title as such for it is not something that can be bought or traded.

In one's heart it is to feel of this feeling within, so that one is to want to implement a new way of which one is to think. Instilling in you this craving to be, for you are to adjust all that you are, in the sensing, the seeing, the doing and the speaking of this self to be. Allow us to offer that in this it will change, hesitant at first but willing all the same.

If you remain in touch and complying to the bold sense of direction that you see to be correct. In here it is that you will feel the freedom of speech, the freedom to act and the freedom of self to arouse up the inner knowing of this that you are.

For you are all bold in your sensing of this to be, it is just the view of self that remains hidden from your sight to be thought of in this way.

Bold in a wanting of self to be is the correctness into which it is that you must see. For it is not of another that is to see this within you.

It is in your own true voice to become that is guiding you into this new state of existence that you feel, it is only in the now of this moment to have that it will be. This one single moment that you sit to breathe, ask and want of to receive, you will feel this change.

The breath that you take is the component of self to believe in all that you see, do, have and believe for in this single breath you bring this inner boldness to the surface to become yours once again.

Author's note:

In this chapter that I was asked to write, in these channelled words offered, I realised that they were not only for you but myself to hear. I sat into this chapter with sadness and a sense of trepidation in my heart. In truth I struggled to hear these words and channellings fluently and clear like all others that have been received. It did not come easy to write these words that appear on the pages that hold them to be read. Why me? I asked, I know nothing about being bold, it defiantly is not me.

For you see I have shunned and still do at times the real world and conversations that I feel directed at me. Hiding away from the questioning eyes and living a life of peace and quiet and becoming recluse like was exactly where I felt the most me. I felt into this a struggle from within, for in my eyes to see and mind to think I was not bold if anything quite the opposite I would think of myself to be. In all aspects of my life and I'm sure you all will have many stories like mine to be shared. And when these stories are spoken of in an honesty, they will open your heart from within a little more. It is in these moments and they are exactly that, just single moments in this time to be spoken of to be heard, that ones such as us are to reveal all that we hold deep into self not wanting to review or speak about. Better to stay quiet, unsaid and hidden.

Am I, not right? This is what it appears in this human to think of all that I am. For you see I am not **Bold**, or I never thought of myself as, to be living a lie and to think that I am, is something that I must speak. My voice was always little and small, I never spoke out loud or out of line, or felt allowed to speak my truth that I wanted so desperately of it to be heard. Many human emotions and feelings I have attached to this sense of inadequacy's and fleeting moments that were to weigh heavy in me when I wished that I could've spoke my truth and in what I really wanted to say. It is in this love of myself that I continued to ask to receive and in this I did, hearing my voice so confidently in the words that spirit spoke. I cherish into each passing moment that I am to be offered these unbiased feelings of love that I am to be confident into this that I am.

I will grow always and most importantly allow into this space that is mine to feel, it's opening becomes mine to sit within. So, don't be too hard upon oneself when you are to feel a clash from within in the suggesting of bold to begin. Let it be offered here to say it is a challenge in our lives that the many of us have become accustomed to hearing of this that we be and think that we are not. In this singular moment of self-thought to be that we make a promise to ourselves, to allow for us to become unwilling to hear words and voices that are spoken of untruths that we have talked of and into this that we have become, but are not. So, it is in here that I sat to write this chapter, that I grew, and I hope that you do too. We are all the same you and I and the ones that ignite us from inside.

It is just that in their very special way, crystal clear it appears that they see us, this that we are the boldest that we have ever been. So, into this I listened to hear the word's that were spoken through me to receive.

I hope that when we meet, I see what you see in me. My **BOLD** to glow for I know that it is my wish to see me and you, **BOLD** together, our boldness glowing, touching and creating a newer, truer version of this that we are. To encourage and allow of ourselves and others to be this that is to become the clearer way to see in the all that we are and the all that we BE.

I could never see myself in this way, we hear you say.

When one is to doubt of the pure existence that dwells within, divinely sitting in her presence of this that she is to be. One allows fear in self to be the ruler, allowing mistrust and the inability to see of this glow from within and becomes deaf to hear of all that she has to offer to you.

Quietly one is to sit for this voice does not appear to talk boldly at first, this we are to speak. She is to be encouraged and guided by those of us that are to love you deeply with such an intention of self to be willing to feel of us once more. It is to be said that this boldness has been yours all along, but in the explicit choosing of these life's to be led and lived ones such as yourselves in these human forms that you have chosen to undertake, it is to be felt from the external viewing of self that earthly life has interfered into your thoughts of self to be.

Believe when we offer that the truer you, the brighter you, the bigger you has never felt this way and has stood tall and strong from within always seeing you in the absolute best you are to be.

CHAPTER 12

SACRED HEART

It is in here that one must sit in relation to the sacred heart that is to be ever prominent within. It is in here that we are to offer that one is to feel the human heart some what scared to be revealed in this space that you request to sit. It is the physical heart, the trying too hard heart to be of this that you are not that one will often see. It is in this offering to many individuals that you are to see that this heart of yours you are to think of as to give to them. Of this you are not. The want and needs of the physical beating heart strives within you to want you to give itself to another. But it is in this the humble heart that was conceived out of this that is to be the consciousness that is yours to be seen is only in a want for you to be the true recipient of this magical heart space to be. It is to be surrounded by this eternal peace and in our seeing thoughts of this to be it will always be held , comforted and relaying back to us the energy that it must, to find of us in this sensing of this that we are to be. You are to determine your thoughts in this way if you are to think of another as yours to be and not of another than it is to be the physical heart that is having her way.

But when one feels the urge to sit and find peace within self before she is to think of another in a certain way, this is to be an offering of the sacred heart that speaks for her voice is soft yet confident in all that she has to say. Her music or sound of notes in love that are to channel from within you will hear not in fear but only of a loving sound that is your god voice from within that is to speak for you to hear.

Sacred is this heart to feel for it is of a must that you want to acknowledge of all that we do witnessing our sensing of yourself to be of us. In here it is to be felt the rhythm of this sacred spot to vibrate from within offering you the space to sit, to feel, to calm and love all that you seek refuge in. You are knowing of this tune for it is yours to vibrate into and in this knowing of your own personal song, your heart song this it is, is the feeling that one is to get to sway and move longingly into this space that you are to create. Sacred knowing's that are to run deep, long lines of wisdom that you have cherished of which to keep. You will find these here as memories from afar ruling within your heart from the times so long ago in this place of recall you are to remember in the divine that you are. Focused intently upon oneself you are to be for it is in this song, this voice only of love that the sacred heart is to emerge, willing and confident in all that you shall appear.

A loving space is required of yours to desire, and in only the space that you see it to be. For your space to want is only in a need of you to think it as, let it be yours in all that you see to trust that you are to want of it to be.

Use these words until your own are to rise:

These are the words given to me in who I am to trust to hear from all that they are to be within this that I am to be.

> *My sacred heart is to evolve. Out of this I am to know; that I am to grow into this heart space once more becoming ever so present in all that I am to act, be and do. She has stood by me this I know, and it is in this getting to know of this space once again that I am to evolve even more. In here it is that I hear her sing and gently speak. For she is my own true sacred heart and of this I am sure. For it is never of another that I am to hear these words that I do, so present, precise and clear within me to hear. I love you. Of this you are me, and in this life I am of you. It is in this us that I be true.*

Sacred hearts you are all to have entwined within this ancient wisdom and physical self that you share into as one a revealing to you this heart that you must trust and never think to disagree.

She knows your paths of many so intently and will ever guide you to these that you are to follow. Listen to her voice and her speech for she is of you as this that is of us to be. We seek of this sacred heart to be just this within you. Ever knowing to see of the truth that is to reside in the all that you see. She is never blinded in sight only if just by the physical that is to think of this earthly view that she sees, misleading her into what is to be right. Your inner voice that attaches and runs internally within this heart that is she in a wanting of all that is within to be correct and in your asking to see of this to be, you will feel this inner glow of bold to shine in all of its glory as though it were of ours.

Your inner sounds and energy that are to be found will not ask you to avoid this love that is yours hopefully already heard to be found, never will it begrudge you in thoughts of this that you are not. For it is of the sacred heart that wants you to breathe into all that you do so that the rhythm of she is felt to vibrate within you.

Breathe deep my sweet loves even with uncertainty if it may begin to start like this for the wanting that is to become will help you into every breath that you're to take.

Let your breath connect you into this heart space that is love to be found so easily within. Let the sound of noise to disappear from the thinking mind that so often overrules you into a sense of this love not to be.

Your breath is your divine path to within that you hold in this heart space to feel as you allow of this breath to open in you a sensing of which it is to begin.

For in the knowing of the beginning not to be so true for you are all into and upon this journey that begun many moons ago, you have already travelled far.

But it is in just this single breath that you are to wish to enter this state of peace to be. You will connect in the deepest of levels of all that is to feel within you to be free. Sensing of self in this space is difficult we offer to you that it may seem, but be encouraged by self in all that she is to just breathe for that often is the hardest task that one shall allow of themselves to do.

Knowing of the physical breath that it appears to just do this job to keep the movement within the physical form stopping. Pushing air here to there and allowing of all that is to need this way to be accepting of it naturally.

But in the hidden breath, the one that you all have chosen to forget, this breath of patience, love and never regret it shall find you eager to accept. Ever so slowly this breath will grow taking over your thoughts of this that you should do. Be kind in asking of this breath to be for in her it is attached to thee.

The rulers of all that you see, the true seer of all that you are to feel and the ever-knowing love that is to guide you intuitively into this that you must. Feel not to fight of this breath for in her ability to see, to hear from this sacred heart that is attached and combined in ever loving thought of this to be mine you will settle into a rhythm all of your own. Knowing that you have felt this space as it is to be yours to sit and not of another's to describe.

It is in this knowing that only the heart shall see. That you will find all of me and in this me it is that you are to be of, for you are the rhythm that is to remain intact always complete full of this love that is to be the ever guiding space of the all that you are to see. Open your eyes wide inside to be greeted by the sacred heart to offer this to you for you will sit in wonderment and awe as how beautiful it is that she be. Let your conversations with her rise and fill you with success and a knowing of this that loves you without detest or judgement of what appears, she hears all that you wish to speak and in what it is that you don't. Feel this beauty within to be complete, fully filled and content within this human that you be for it is only of the holder of this such heart to be that you will truly come to appreciate this creature that you be, loving and in the grace of thee this is us to be seen.

Fear not of rejection it is to be said for the heart that is yours painted and clothed in the heart song that is yours will never acknowledge such a word, to remember that in your space not ours you only see this in this time. But it is of you dear ones that have forgotten you all have been in this space that you are yet to remember again this that you are. Rejoice into this knowing upon once it is to be felt for you will need never of another to uncover this within you to allow for their thoughts or speech to be true. For it is in here that you will hear of all that is to reign true within you.

This sensing of your sacred heart is yours and only in the deepest of wanting's will it be felt in a single breath for you to take and to relate to the heart with hope that you will feel the shift that is to generate an opening from within. Feel as this loving space trances you from within, in this we offer that you must listen, for she is appreciative to your being of this that you are and will not willingly ask of this on her own.

It is to be you that is to take the initiative and ask in a wanting felt so strong, that you will know that it was heard to be felt. See of this big love that is to sit into your heart for it knows no discord or distrust in only of you it is to trust that the ever knowing wisdom that rises from within will be yours to see.

Human time in that one is to think, is to be found to be ill relevant in here that we sit with you as the receiver of ALL that we be to offer.

Limitless we are with no restrictions or constraints regarding this time that you speak of as not enough. Sit with encouragement spoken from within and this time of yours to choose, will be exactly as it shall be.

For it is to be simply just this of us, that is to be easily found within you to be.

What if sacred is not for me? The word sacred feels like religious I should be.

Is it not of a religious sensing that we are in need to be seen, for it is only of the viewer that looks at us in this way that we shall be? In the thinking of oneself to be not of this way that is to be spoken of by us as okay. You are in right the you that you be and in the thinking of us to be received only in a house of religion, temple or prayer is usually where we are to lose the many of you there, for you see this is of what it is that we wish to say. That in the all that are to be in the ever-knowing god as such that we be you are all ever present and in this completeness that be. For it is in here that your gods, idols, masters and many that you strive to be of, sit with us to hear. For in the voices of many this we are to speak but in the only way to hear it is in the voice that lays deep within that you are to hear only of this voice that is to speak and it is yours that you are to speak the words that we are to be.

For in a religion or following as such to be we are not. It is in the choosing to see this as us to know that it is heard rather than felt to truly know, by those that feel the urge to express their own thoughts into which it is to know in them of us to be. Let all that grace your path with the thoughts as such of us to be. Be just this to be offered they are correct within themselves as they are to see us to be. We seek not to change their view for in their own space into which it is that it will enter they will surely change their minds eye as to what it is that they are to see, their own heart will feel into the true wanting of us to be. We are not only for the high and mighty, the rich or the do gooder's it would seem, for we are in the all of every single being that is to exist upon this planet and the many that are too far away to be found.

So, religion is just a title as such that you in this human form love to gather in and entrust within a certain knowing of whom it is that is to be seen as the one true king among you all to be. Leave off the crown and badges of such to be, so to speak and sit amongst yourselves and let love spell out to you the ruler that is to be found within. For in this we offer for you to hear that you are the true rulers of all that is to be in the accepting of self to be found once more in this continual movement of eternalness that we all are.

How do I trust that what I am seeing, and feeling is to be true?

We seek not of you to believe into us if you don't. Our seeing of you will always be true in this place that we sit. You are extraordinary to us this creature that you have chosen to be. Finding yourself upon this planet as such to be called Earth and it is a must within the most of you to forget of this that we be. So, in this you are to feel that one must be earning of your trust and this is proven within that it shall be. You need not fear that we will not hear in all that you ask to speak. For in this that we hear we hear your voices timid and lost in the searching of us and when you feel the inclination from within the human mind and physical heart to wish for something more to be, this is when you will feel the slight stirrings of a beginning of trust in this that we be. We have no need to ask for you to be trusting in us, for you are to realise in the depths of your entire being to be that upon the sight of us to feel, to see you will want not of any other to be the offeror of this so called trust. If we could offer here it is not of trust that we speak of it to offer for in this place and it is to exist is only to be known as a love so grand that you could never completely understand of it to be seen as the almighty that is within you. In here it is that only love in trust is spoke and you will be the receiver of this to be yours to know whole heartedly once you ask of it to be. Many of you have asked this we see; **how do I know that you are what I see?** In this we are to offer, surrender to your willing heart to be the rememberer of this that you once all were to be and in this you will feel the resistance slip away from the human that holds you captive to the sensing that isn't physical and cannot be seen in the human way to see. Know of our presence you all shall again for you are to feel in us this that we are to be you in every way.

I want to see but do not, Why?

You all see of this that is to be in the way that you are looking and often it is this way to be. Notice in the way that you look for what it is that you want.

How do you see of what it is that is to surround you?
Do you glance over things quickly to judge?
Are you critical of self and others to witness?
Is it not of yours to see in this way that you do?
Is it of what you are really wanting to see?
Is it in others that you choose to see?
Is it of your wanting of it to be?

Rate your thoughts of your seeing abilities; Is what you see being judged by the blinded physical self that sits in conformity to witness or is it from within this space that is to see clearly and knowingly of all that you are to see.

Be oblivious to us and in this it is that you won't see to know of the all that we are. That is your choice to be yours to make. We sense all of you and hear in this that you speak, if you are wanting then we are willing to be. One must view only of what it is that they are wanting and know of this in truth to see, for you are the wise seer of all that is to be yours. Let go of visions of self not to be worthy and investigate this space that you will create deep in imagination and fantasy with ease to see all that you desire to have. You are all to evolve out of this that you are so to know yourself as the seer of love that you are, you will see this miraculous loving being in which it is that you are, and in here it is that you will truly see "I".

In the sensing of self to be, you will seek out the true voice of love that is to rule from within this that you are. In one's thoughts of self, they will generate the obvious sights to see for in these thoughts of self to be lay many ideas and suggestions that are to be offered by another.

See of them to be only of a screen that is allowed to project an image of this to be, for you are not to wonder in all at how it is meant to be. See only of this open space that is to be yours to enter into, no parting of curtains or veils to lift or invisible lines to step over. For you are already in our offerings of this that we be, you see only of what it is to appear before thee so in the hard looking that is such you are unable to focus on the invisible that is. In here it is that we sit watching you all in love in this experience of you to be of. For you all generated into self it would seem looking over your shoulders at what should have been. Live not another moment in this regret of what is not. For in here it is that we are to sit with you to be the internal being of light and love that you are, we are just the guiders from above as some would say of the very being of love that you are. Feel as the reigns of self-control are allowed to be dismantled and laid down for if you are to understand of this that we are, then one must be willing in her sensing of us to be the everything inside of you that is.

For our space that we inhabit is expansive this we have said and in all that is to sit here upon these words that are about to be said you will feel the energy flow direct in regards to all that you are of neglect within one self.

See not of us to fulfill you for you are fulfilled eternally and in this that we are is the strength we see in you. You are creatures of habit this is to be said for you are in a continual search within self to be looking for what it appears to be incorrect and in this asking of self to be helped. We see not of this within thee, it is only of the light that we are to see. Allow of your glance to be one of no hesitation upon spots of this that you are to see, for to dwell here is to feel the pull from all that you are to think of yourself to be. It is in this forming of opinions of this that you think is to be discovered within and from afar that you will feel the steady numbing of this physical self that you are. You are focused to intently into this that we are. Soften your hold, dial down all intensity of thoughts to be and relax within to hear the sweet talk of this that you are. We whisper gently to you and in your quite head you will certainly hear these words to be said.

IN ALL THAT YOU ARE, YOU WILL BE.

CHAPTER 13

JOY

It is a joyous occasion is it not when one is to feel of a certain happiness within that cannot be explained to all that are to ask. For the movement within this that be you is to steer you in this sense of satisfaction of all that you have become. Becoming steady in thoughts and a willingness to be this perfect form of such that you are to be.

> *In joy we speak for it is to be found into this life that you are to live in this to be your now.*

All of life that you live within this steady hum of joy running in the background for you to hear will steel your thoughts on how your life should be. In joy one can only see the true light into all that they are to see. In Joy you will witness a change from within from this that thought she couldn't but now sees herself as **I can**.

Joy, we hear when spoken of is a word of cheer in your language as such to speak.

One is lost to joy if they are to be thrust into a situation that does not agree with the speaker of all that be that is to reside within. Let this joy grow to expand in a wholeness of fun, love and expansion of self to be for you are entitled of this to be felt within you to see. Billowing out of you in a sensing of self to be only to want to receive of this joyous momentum that is to be yours to witness.

It is in this joy that you are to possess exclusively yours for no other is your bold, your love, your ruler, your light.

It is all your own doing this we say.

We watch as you grow day by day moments in this to be your time, sensing within of this joy to begin in the opening of such that you be. Feel as you are to catch yourself smiling in the simple pleasures of life and moments to enjoy realising that this is what love is all about. You see things differently from most and in this you are happy to quote, my life is full and in this I find joy for it is of my asking of such to be. Allow for voice to commute to us in this that you want for all that is to be comes out of a feeling of joy, happiness and love to……

SIMPLY

We sense into you this that you are to feel as you are being capable and confident in the true sensing of this self to be. Feel as you are to open internally to the deepest of love that is to spark within to ignite this innerness that is to be the true driver within you into this life that you are to be seeing into. Feel as she is to know of all that you are to become into this occasion as such that it is to present to you to see clearly into. For if you are allowing of these inner eyes to see of what your sacred heart is to feel, then and only then will you cherish every moment of contention to be seen into as an occasion to deliver these feelings of joy to arise for you to see intently into.

Joy is yours to be, to do and to have it is not of another that one must rely on to offer this to you. See yourself as your own giver of this joy to become, for only you the true bearer of this light that is eternally yours is to know of the complete and absolute love and joy that you are to hold within. Let it feel free to roam within your everyday thinking thoughts of this that you are and all that you glance your physical eyes upon to witness to see. For to see of only joy one must realise of the beautiful you within me that you all are to become again into this that we are of the eternal asking of self to become.

Your joy is mine to see, for if one is to only look at each other and all that is to be physical and non-physical through eyes that see only JOY, you will see the true picture to which it is that one must see everlastingly and lovingly as the way into this that your world is supposed to....

You are of this joy are you not to know?

In the sensing of self to be allowing to feel of this that you describe as joy to feel. One must be in a wanting to feel that they are to be of this to acknowledge within themselves as a contentment of such to be. For your joy is to be viewed not as another's and in this you are to know of that each and everyone that is to experience of this joy that we speak of is to feel it in their own sensing of this that is to be theirs to feel into. Ones joy as such to you must only be this that you are to feel as yours and not of another's to feel into.

It is our greatest wanting for you to feel into this that you are to be ever complete within so that you are to never need this urge to rise from within to seek of this that you are not, and that you are to always be in this place of willingness to be ever knowing of this

Joy

you are to be.

IN EVERY MOMENT
TO BE, I AM.

The divineness that lays deeply within
is to be yours to feel is it not?

Let it be offered to you to hear into this that
you are, is to be found only in the truthful
voice that is yours to speak into and of.

It is of this voice that you are to reign supreme within
and will not be in the need to search for the beauty of
this that you are to be realised into.   Take care of your
thoughts to be this that you are for in your words to
speak and thoughts to think you are the most powerful
creator of the all that be in this that is you to see.

In ones asking, to receive in this that is to be heard in all its truth and correctness that is to be felt as an internal understanding of this that you are.

Ones such as yourself will be resistant to hear of such these words that are to exclaim to ones that are to listen, to feel into this that you are, **Grand.**

For it is not of the human race typically to accept these words such as great, big, loved, complete and magnificent to be heard in the trueness of which it is that they are spoken by us to you all to hear into. This we are to offer to you to hear of this, believe into this being of love that you are for she is your greatest admirer of all that you be and she is the true knower of truth in this that you are to become once more to see yourself as perfection to be.

"When ones such as yourself are to be willing, the universal loves become yours to feel into once more".

"THE BEAUTIFUL YOU WITHIN ME"

Is to be offered here by us to speak into, that in all that you are you will be of this that is to rule supreme within this that is to be your ever guiding love for this being that you are.

And it is of our greatest intentions for this to be heard that you are to truly know of the greatness that lays within the all of you that are to realise your self's to be.

Much love in receiving of this to be felt, to be heard, to be spoken. I am always of gracious heart and place to be allowing of all that is needed to be heard to offer.

www.ingramcontent.com/pod-product-compliance
Lightning Source LLC
Chambersburg PA
CBHW070306010526
44107CB00056B/2507